LOVING THE CHRIST IN YOU

GEORGE A. MALONEY, S.J., is the founder of Contemplative Ministries and the author of many books on prayer and spirituality.

BARBARA J. ROGERS-GARDNER is the author of *In the Center*, a spiritual autobiography.

To

Lucia Van Ruiten,

with gratitude

LOVING THE CHRIST IN YOU

A Spiritual Path to Self-Esteem

GEORGE A. MALONEY

and

BARBARA J. ROGERS-GARDNER

A Meyer-Stone Book
CROSSROAD • NEW YORK

1991

The Crossroad Publishing Company
370 Lexington Avenue, New York, NY 10017

© 1987 by George A. Maloney
and Barbara J. Rogers-Gardner

Cover design: Evans-Smith & Skubic

Cover photo: Mark H. Gardner

Manufactured in the United States of America

Library of Congress Cataloging-in-Publication Data

Maloney, George A., 1924–
  Loving the Christ in you: a spiritual path to self-esteem
  George A. Maloney and Barbara J. Rogers-Gardner.
      p.   cm.
  Includes bibliographies.
  ISBN 0-940989-15-8
  1. Self-respect – Religious aspects – Christianity.   2. Spiritual
life.   I. Rogers Gardner, Barbara J., 1935-   II. Title.
BV4647.S43M34 1987
  248.4 – dc19   87-18431
                                                                         CIP

Contents

Introduction

What does it mean to have Christ at the core of our being? To live in the state of Christ-consciousness? First of all, it means to know that we were made in the image of God and are temples of the Holy Spirit. We must also realize, however, that we have lived our lives for the most part as if we were anything but God's. We spend our lives building up and supporting an ego that creates its own world and then suffers guilt because it has usurped the role of God. The ego creates without love, lives in the prison of self-consciousness, then fears that if it dies, we will die with it. This book is about the great mistake of believing *our ego is us*.

To live in Christ-consciousness is to be aware that divinity is our inheritance. The death of who we thought we were begins the life of who we really are. Distinguishing our false self from our true self, the Christ-in-us, is the main purpose of our life on earth. The thesis of this book is that through self-emptying love we are reborn into a life that unifies us with all humankind as its history unfolds the plan of God.

Both Christian faith and Christian practice are part of that unfolding. Each chapter of the book is followed by an exercise intended to help you embody Christ's teachings in

1

your everyday life. The more consistently and often you repeat the exercises, the more you will benefit from your reading. But no mere study of another's words can effect a radical transformation of our lives. "Pray without ceasing," Jesus told us. *Loving the Christ in You* is dedicated to helping you make your whole existence a prayer, so that you can become continuously aware of the Christ who lives in you, the Christ in whom we live, move, and have our being.

Our Christian vision of reality begins with a view of our brokenness and alienation from God, from our true selves, from other human beings, and from nature. God's creation of us as a divine image and likeness Gen. 1:26) placed us above all other creatures and in harmony with them. Our selfish egos disrupted that harmony, blaming others for self-caused pain, mistaking the effect for the cause, forgetting that devils as well as divinity are within us. But despite our attempts to hide in our darkness, God's great love went on shining upon creation like the sun, giving warmth and light.

God came among us in the person of Jesus Christ, through whom the Spirit poured living waters that flood the whole cosmos. God's forgiveness and at-one-ment with us through the death and resurrection of Jesus release divine, uncreated, loving energies within us, healing the wound of our separation from God and from all that God made for us. The name of Christ, the Logos that sang the creation of the world, is in our mouths, giving us birth all over again, this time in the Holy Spirit. Our new Eden is the whole universe; our new law is love.

The last four centuries have revolutionized the view

of reality held by the human race since the neolithic age began. For untold thousands of years human beings had hunted with rough stone weapons; for thousands more they worked the land. In this long night of slavery, Christianity offered a bright glimpse of personal worth, personal growth, a mature I–Thou relationship with God and the whole human family. As Karl Jaspers wrote, it was the first of three great transitions in human history.

After the Middle Ages, the second great transition took place. Christendom discovered the laws of physics and began to harness the impersonal energy of machines. And so the human race was catapulted into a new dimension of awareness, a liberation from brute labor, that for the first time in history made it possible for ordinary people to cultivate their bodies, minds, and spirits. The "enlightened" age that ignited technology restricted human consciousness to one side of the brain, the left, or analytical, side. In this scientific age, then, only sensory reality, with its extensions through instruments, has been taken seriously.

The third great transition, happening at this moment, is the planetization of humanity, which both promises and demands a further expansion of human consciousness beyond cultural or national boundaries. For as the world becomes increasingly one, what happens to every human being or every continent is crucial to the survival and development of us all. Jaspers insists on the unified planet: "There is no longer anything outside it."[1]

Contemporary physicists have proved that the view of reality taught by the old-fashioned science of the materialists is as fanciful as that of the ancients, who thought that the only elements were earth, air, fire, and water. The table that our senses tell us is solid, the new physicists tell us is almost entirely empty space. We think we see lines meeting in the distance but they touch only in our eyes and minds; to another viewer in the next town, they are still parallel. As Einstein discovered, what we in our self-centeredness think is absolute, in the cosmic perspective is merely relative.

Neurologist Karl Pribram has shown us that our idea of reality is only a map of the territory, not the territory itself, with rivers to wet the feet in, mountains to climb. Our brain filters and reduces the vast amount of data received, selecting, constructing, and imposing its own beliefs on incoming stimuli. Emotions, desires, and abstract concepts also play a role in our construction of reality. Without our capacity to create our own world, we would not survive, but because of it, we are subject to illusion. In the educational process of the Western child, the senses and concepts based on sensory knowing are taught exclusively. Aboriginal children in Australia, on the other hand, actually see and converse with spirits. Our "reality" is illusion for the multitudes of the East; their reality is to us a dream. Clearly, the senses are not a reliable guide to absolute reality, for they give us only a small fraction of what exists and they distort even that.

During the past twenty years, altered states of consciousness have allowed us to experience the new, nonsensory reality discovered by modern physics. Stanley Krippner describes twenty such states, including dreaming, hypnotic and hypnopompic phenomena (states prior to and after sleep), hyper-alertness, lethargy, rapture, daydreaming, meditation, trance, stupor, coma, and expanded consciousness.[2] When an outworn reality-construct breaks up, the result is the break-up of old habits developed to perceive and act on that construct. The dehabituation process, according to Dr. Arthur Deikman, comes about through altering the state of consciousness.[3] But for the Christian, the breakdown of an outworn system of processing reality is only half the battle. We must construct a new and more accurate model of the universe.

Consciousness researchers explain that the breakdown of old systems and the substitution of new ones take place in two ways. The first demolishes all structures, as does Zen meditation, in favor of a "Now-Moment" in which we are totally aware of the present in its cosmic fullness and of nothing else. Claudio Naranjo and Robert E. Ornstein write of the meditational approach to grasping reality: "Meditation is a summoning up within oneself of a state of being that is not something to be created but our deepest reality. For this reality of ours to awaken, on the other hand, 'we' must stand aside."[4] The setting aside of that "we," or rather of that "I," is what the exercises in this book attempt to bring about. But getting rid of the ego is only the beginning.

The second way human beings dehabituate their responses to artificial structures is to replace the old structures with new ones, which Thomas Kuhn, in *The Structure of Scientific Revolutions,* argues is the method of science. Such a view insists that we must have some collective vision of reality, not relying solely on personal inspiration of the moment. The love of God, which holds the universe together, is for Christians that collective vision. Acceptance of the vision in the everyday living of our lives we call faith.

Let us follow through history the growth of faith in our vision of God as love, seeing how it accords with our personal development as spiritual beings, seeing with new eyes, hearing with new ears, the single word that brought forth the universe and all that is in it. We will understand that the development of faith rises in a spiral, recapitulating all the levels that preceded the present one. The history of God's interaction with human time and God's transformation of our lives are two sides of the same coin. In the words of Blaise Pascal, "We know the truth not only through reason, but also through our heart."[5] We know both through the collective journey of the race in time and through our personal experience of trust in God.

Our spiritual history, after the dead-end of Eden, was opened when Abraham was called to leave ancient Sumer in search of the Promised Land, the promised state of interior wholeness. He left the infancy of the spiritual primitive, who remains unconscious of personal identity, responsibility, and transfiguration, and headed west toward the sunset, toward the eventual full maturity of the human race, Teilhard de Chardin's Omega-Point. God had promised Abraham that his seed would be as many as the stars. Yet God also asked him in a test of faith to offer up his only child. As Abraham's knife was in mid-air, God intervened:

Abraham, Abraham....
Do not raise your hand against the boy....
Do not harm him,
        for now I know you fear God.
You have not refused me your son, your only son.
                                    [Gen. 22:11–13]

God's plan to establish a covenant with the human race could now unfold because Abraham kept faith. At the point of Abraham's knife, at the point of his obedience, we ourselves began our spiritual evolution. We would be Abraham's seed, and like Abraham we would be channels through which the world would be blessed and transformed.

As Moses led the descendants of Abraham out of captivity in Egypt, they experienced God's love in the emptiness of the desert, knowing God as tender and compassionate (Exod. 34:6). They were children of a family, and like us as children, lived by the rules of a tribe, rarely conscious of personal, private life. Yet the implications of a personal God gave the Hebrews the beginnings of self-knowledge, foreign to the experience of anonymous neighboring masses caught up in primitive nature worship. John B. Cobb suggests that a "vague mode of understanding emerged among the Hebrews, which can best be pointed to in our vocabulary by the idea of person."[6] What is important about this stage in the spiritual evolution of the race is that the "thou shalt" of the Ten Commandments makes the human person morally responsible to God and to the community. Human beings are are no longer children.

The adolescence of the Jewish people took place in Babylon, still a symbol for decadence and sexual sin, the place where the individual must come of age without the old tribal supports of childhood. As youths coming into puberty are disturbed by changes in body and mind and leave the parental rule to seek their own identity, so the Jewish people, having lost temple and homeland and living among pagan strangers, were forced to develop an identity beyond that of the tribe and its law. The prophet Jeremiah called his exiled people to a circumcision of the heart, to return love for love: "Circumcise yourselves for Yahweh:

off with the foreskin of your hearts" (Jer. 4:4). Jeremiah asked the people to confront themselves honestly, to repent of their sins, and to change their way of life so they could experience the forgiving love of God.

> Then when you call to me,
>   and come to plead with me,
>   I will listen to you.
> When you seek me you shall find me,
>   when you seek me with all your heart:
>   I will let you find me.
>
> [Jer. 29:12–14]

The cry from the prophets is: Be converted. Turn to Yahweh in a decision of your heart. Not sacrifice, but obedience is what the Lord would have (see 1 Sam. 15:22; Amos 5:21–24; Hos. 6:6; Isa. 1:1–11; Jer. 7:21–23). Individual responsibility is part of a dawning I –Thou relationship between God and the individual. Eichrodt, the Old Testament scholar, writes: "The man to whom God's demand comes is recognized as a person, an *I*, who cannot be represented or replaced by any other."[7] The static security of the tribal existence as an end in itself was cracking. Instead of the Old Covenant, written on tablets of stone, God was calling the Jewish people to a New Covenant written on the hearts of individuals.

> Deep within them I will plant my Law,
>   writing it on their hearts.
> Then I will be their God
>   and they shall be my people.
>
> [Jer. 31:33–34]

The Jewish people were no longer children, but mature, responsible adults. The human person had begun to emerge.

What happened to the Jewish people in the Exile happens to all of us as we grow toward physical, psychological, and spiritual maturity. We become adolescents and break away from old authorities in order to find ourselves as free, morally responsible individuals. In the process, however, we lose that sense of oneness with the world around us that made infancy and childhood so joyful. Alone, no longer a "we," I seek the "I" of others, the "I" of God. But my own "I" has swollen to such a size that I can no longer see around it.

I have moved from external authority into myself, discovering a new authority and power — my own separate ego. Like the Jews in exile and the confused adolescent, now that I have found myself, I must struggle in my isolation to find God. Former communal services, rituals, pious practices, and even personal prayer seem to be obsolete, meaningless. The human being at this stage is struggling to say "I" to God and yet cannot quite hear God's "Thou."

If we, along with the Jewish people in exile, remained only on the *I*-level of autonomy, we would never grow. We would never unite with the human family, but would remain separated egos. The coming of Christ allowed us to move beyond the egotistic level of consciousness, in which we are "chosen people," and into full humanity. Mircea Eliade writes:

> If Abraham's faith can be defined as "for God everything is possible," the faith of Christianity implies that everything is also possible for man . . . (Mark 11: 22–24). Faith in this context, as in many others, means absolute emancipation from any kind of natural "law" and hence the highest freedom that man can

imagine: freedom to intervene even in the ontologi-
cal constitution of the universe. It is, consequently, a
pre-eminently creative freedom.[8]

Jesus Christ leads us into this mature, creative freedom,
unhindered by the limitations of infantile demands, ego-
tism, or human laws designed to subject the individual to
the tribe.

We are drawn into the I–Thou bond with God and
with the whole body of creation, beyond distinctions of
Jew or Gentile, servant or free, male or female (Gal. 3:28).
This new level of consciousness is rooted in the *other* that
brings forth the *we* in mutual self-giving, not only to each
other but to us all, "for we are members of his Body, of
his flesh, and of his bones" (Eph. 5:30).

Jesus did not come to destroy the Jewish faith but
to fulfill it. He not only spoke of the Father, as had the
prophets, but was one with the Father, as Jesus promised
we would be one in him, branches of the vine. Not the
individual then, but the fulfilled being-in-community is the
goal of the evolution of consciousness and of faith. We are
now carried in the womb of the world with all our brothers
and sisters, the family of God, and reborn with them.

The miracle of new life did not come about by our own
effort, any more than our first birth did. Mind-expanding
programs might lead us erroneously to believe that alone
we can change our perception of reality, that the power to
do it is within us like a fruit contained in the seed. But
Christianity teaches, and history demonstrates, that we
cannot do it ourselves.

We have to be shown how to give ourselves away in
love. We need a savior. Our proud egos must bow down

in an act of trust, become as little children. Unless we surrender to God, we will be stuck in our separated selves until we die.

Through faith in Jesus' resurrection, we are raised to the full meaning of individual freedom and to unity with God's body across the planet.

Like Abraham sacrificing his son in faith, Jesus believed so totally in God's love that he was free to forgive the Roman soldiers who killed him, even to lay down his life for them in love, widening the faith of Abraham into a cosmic covenant, excluding no one.

Before he died, Jesus acted out in ritual form the covenant that began at Mamre when Abraham offered his sacrifice, completely surrendering to God. The night before Jesus died, he shared himself as food and drink with his friends. In prefiguring his death on the cross the next day, he said,

> This is my body
> which will be given for you;
> do this as a memorial of me....
> This cup is the new covenant
> in my blood
> which will be poured out for you....
> [Luke 22:19–20]

Dying on the cross was God's ultimate intervention in human history. In that act God's self-giving to humankind, to the whole universe, was total.

A new level of consciousness opens to those who accept the risen Christ as present within them through the Holy Spirit. St. Paul described the new I–Thou level of consciousness in these words:

> And for anyone who is in Christ
>   there is a new creation;
> The old creation has gone
>   and now the new one is here.
> It is all God's work.
>
>   [2 Cor. 5:17–18]

We have become the chalice of the world, empty to the Spirit, who re-creates the cosmos by filling us with Spirit.

When the Holy Spirit filled the disciples, they shifted to a higher level of consciousness than when they were under the Law. Dr. Herbert Richardson expresses this new awareness, this fearlessness of death itself, in the following words:

> There was a higher kind of Life above and beyond the life of nature and history. There was a Life that was not subject to mutability and death and decay, a Life whose structure and order pervaded every biological and historical entity and caused them to be alive.[9]

Jesus, living within his disciples, released his Spirit, who shaped them into members capable of love and self-sacrifice for their one Body. "The whole group of believers was united, heart and soul. No one claimed for his own use anything that he had, as everything they owned was held in common" (Acts 4:32).

Without the example and presence of the risen Christ, we would remain lonely individuals, trying to raise ourselves by a bootstrap operation to a new arc of the evolutionary spiral, something that 5,000 years of human history have not been able to do. We now carry within us the Teacher of teachers and need no guru to control us from outside. Christians, whose living guide is within them, are free individuals, under the domination of no human being.

Our freedom is the responsibility, laid on us by love, to put aside our false self in order to live in Christ, our true self, in whom we love and serve all human beings, for they wear Christ's face.

> Now this Lord is the Spirit, and where the Spirit of the Lord is, there is freedom, and we, with our unveiled faces reflecting like mirrors the brightness of the Lord, all grow brighter and brighter as we are turned into the image that we reflect.... [2 Cor. 3:18]

Every breath we breathe is now a prayer; we live in the burning bush and breathe fire. Together, as a community, we approach the altar of God, who is the consuming fire (Heb. 12:29), with childlike hope that all the sins of our past will be burned and that God's life will rise in us like spring sap in a tree.

Around the Communion table this family gathers and opens its mouth to be fed. In taking Christ into us, we become the living flesh and blood of the earth; we become rocks, rivers, inseparable from each other and from the world into which we are woven. We are healed not only in our own minds, but in the whole body — in the family of God. Their flesh, their blood is ours; we have received them in receiving God, just as we love God in loving them. As God feeds us with Christ, so we feed God to the world. In our Communion we draw the power and glory of the cosmic Christ into the heart of matter, even as he is evolving the universe into his Body. "I am the Alpha and the Omega," says the Lord God, who is, who was, and who will be ... " (Rev. 1:8). Into the timeless, spaceless Trinity, we carry our bit of earth, the clay from which we were formed, shaped by the Potter into a vessel fit for living water, fit for light.

What we are, what we have become, is good in the sight of God. No matter how broken we might be, one thing is sure: that even as we are, God loves us with an unconditional love. By such love our broken fragments are gathered together and transformed into a whole. By trust we are both healed and opened to love at a single stroke. Not by our brains or our wills or even our good behavior (Eph. 2:8) do we come alive in God, but by a conscious letting go of all we once thought or wished we were. Having struggled to become grown, self-sufficient men and women, we must come full circle to become newborn children again, in order to complete our destiny, to become at once wise and innocent. In the sacred, transformative ritual of Communion, we are fed like babies at the breast of God. Brothers and sisters together in one Body, we are transformed by this feeding into the Christ of the manger, the Christ of the cross, the Christ of the empty tomb. Into every thirsty cell and tissue of our body's dust flows the life of God.

The work of the Spirit is to join us with God, to give us a common consciousness with the whole of creation. That is the Good News Jesus told us to tell the world by our love, by our lives. Teilhard de Chardin urges us to "try with God's help to perceive the connection between physical and natural which binds your labor with the building of the kingdom...."[10] What we do during our lives echoes in the whole universe; we ourselves are the song of God.

Our world is charged with the grandeur of God. God's loving energies beat inside each atom, each molecule, saturating the universe, nourishing it in one holy continuous communion. In this transfigured world we walk God-like, as loved children (Eph. 5:1–2). God's love is all around us like the air we breathe.

It often hurts to be alive, to be in a body. At first we fight painfully to breathe into our flesh and bones the Spirit of God, as the newborn struggles for air. But we were made to be a soul married to flesh. If we throw away our body, where are we going to live? And so we begin to take care of our own incarnation, passing through our daily life with great respect, for God is in us. Nothing is more extraordinary, more sacred, than this small miracle, our lives.

Coming home to God, coming full circle, we find ourselves on familiar ground — the core of our own consciousness. We are where we belong, where we always were, only now our eyes are wide open, and here in our hearts we see God.

> We shall not cease from exploration,
> And the end of all our exploring
> Will be to arrive where we started
> And know the place for the first time.[11]

Notes

1. Karl Jaspers, *The Origin and Goal of History* (New Haven: Yale University Press, 1953), p. 140.

2. See Stanley Krippner, "Altered States of Consciousness," in *The Highest State of Consciousness*, ed. John White (Garden City, N.Y.: Doubleday Anchor, 1972), pp. 1–5.

3. Arthur J. Deikman, "Experimental Meditation," in ibid., pp. 203–223, and "Deautomatization and the Mystic Experience" in ibid., pp. 25–46.

4. Claudio Naranjo and Robert E. Ornstein, *On the Psychology of Meditation* (New York: Viking Press, 1971), p. 48.

5. Blaise Pascal, *Les Pensées*, no. 110.

6. John B. Cobb, *The Structure of Christian Existence* (Philadelphia: Fortress Press, 1967), p. 99.

7. Walther Eichrodt, *Man in the Old Testament* (London: SCM, 1966), p. 23.

8. Mircea Eliade, *The Myth of the Eternal Return* (New Haven: Yale University Press, 1971), pp. 160–161.

9. Herbert Richardson, *Nun, Witch, Playmate: The Americanization of Sex* (New York: Harper & Row, 1971), p. 26.

10. Pierre Teilhard de Chardin, *The Divine Milieu*, trans. Bernard Wall (New York: Harper & Row, 1960), pp. 35–36.

11. T. S. Eliot, *Four Quartets* (New York: Harcourt & Brace & Co., 1943), p. 39.

— I —

Human Person, Divine Icon

Before growing up to think and to suffer consequent separation from nature, early human beings lived in an Eden of perpetual childhood. They saw in dreams and spoke in poetry. Genesis pictures the first human beings walking through a garden world like happy children, celebrating each day as though it were their first. All nature was an extension of themselves and they lived in the world like unborn children in the womb. At the same time, they mothered and fathered the life growing around them, as they were mothered and fathered by the God they knew as intimately as they knew themselves.

Human beings were created as mystics, at home in heaven and on earth, drawing no line between the two. They took in the unified field of nature and spirit in one visionary glance and drank living water from the well of that Absolute Being we now call God. Adam and Jesus called this Being "Abba," "Daddy," for they knew God as God was, not as the stranger our thinking, self-centered brains have created. Because they did not separate them-

17

selves from God or God from the world, these first human beings looked at creation and agreed with God that it was good. After the joyful harvest of their days, they danced, then slept and danced again, to the endless music of their dreams.

A poem written in Sanscrit five thousand years ago recalls to us anxious modern men and women that joyful child-self we have locked deep in the labyrinth of our unconscious. In embryonic form, that little child beckons us grown-up human beings into a newness of life possible only if we were to let these powers unfold from within us:

See yourself bestowing your goodness and warmth to all.

Pour out your strength and calm.

Call upon the forces of good to pervade all things.

Reach out beyond knowing and embrace oneness.

Healing as you go, breathe the living word restoring creation.

Share the spiritual fire and let the mystic light of God fill you to overflowing.

Ultimately there is only one truth, one pure blessed reality:

That the powers of love will pervade and overcome all things.

We will rest in utter completion of wonder.

We are not alone, but we are within the same mystical unfolding.

Happy are we only in as far as kindness and vision live within shining outward.

Words are shadows; acts are born of real caring and loving.

A truth in stillness do we share in the moments be-
    yond time,
Fleeting touches of an ultimate total embrace.
Within these things lies the most sacred and simple
    mystery of all:
We are loved, utterly and completely.

Such a being it was that Jesus took on his lap and held
in his arms, saying, "Unless you become as little children,
you will not enter the kingdom of heaven."

After childhood, we became fragmented and separated
from each other. We began to believe that God and the
reality outside us exist only in relation to ourselves, to be
measured only by our small rule. We came to consider
ourselves the center of our cosmos. Building on sand, we
have lost touch with God, the Ground of all being, the
Source, the Beginning and the End.

All things belong to God, but we have taken them as
ours, raping nature, taking it by force as something to be
possessed and used for our own selfish purposes. We judge
the conduct of others as though we were God and refuse
to find any fault in our own. We violently attack others
and project onto them the source of all our problems: our
own desire to take the place of God.

Our technological control over nature has unleashed
our demon into the world around us, and we live in fear
of the fallout from our own bombs. Fear dominates us
and makes us fight the wrong enemy. We have not yet
understood that the enemy whom we confront is us.

Is it not strange that the wealthiest countries are led by
fear and not by generous love? Driven by our insecurities
to accumulate more goods and to enjoy more creature-

comforts, we live in fear that we will lose what we have to thieves, taxes, or inflation. As one wit has said of our time, "Too much ain't enough." Toxic water and air sting the nose and rot the lungs; public mineral resources are being handed over to the wealthy, impoverishing the rest of humankind. Fumes from our machines rise up to cloud the atmosphere with a gaseous shroud that may eventually choke all plant, animal, and human life on planet Earth. Noble humankind, created by God to be little less than a god (Ps. 8:5), becomes a quintessence of dust as we build up bigger walls to separate ourselves from others, the enemies who, we think, are out to destroy us. The real enemy, however, is that false self who gnaws at our insides until we are empty shells.

And we continue to put on masks and play roles before each other, hollow persons who speak in hollow voices, stuffed with the straw of ego, our bones too dry to live. Anxieties and fears increase as we continue to be false to those true selves that might rise like living water from God within us, from the source of Being out of which we sprang, selves that we have never really known. Gabriel Marcel, the French philosopher, quotes Sartre, who looks condescendingly down on the coffeehouse waiter. "For [Sartre]," writes Marcel, "to be the father of a family is always and inevitably to be someone who is playing the father of a family,"[1] while for the simple, uncorrupted man, to be a father as God is a father is to forget both self and fatherhood altogether, dying in order to live and give life.

What was originally meant by God to have been a world both unending in its richness and diversity and a harmonious whole, unified by love, has been distorted into a world seen darkly through the glass of separation and alienation. In the mythopoetic account in the book of Genesis, we are shown how Adam and Eve disobeyed God, taking power into their own hands. A life of self-inflicted pain, of brother killing self and brother, of human beings killing nature in the name of conquest, is the result of that original sin. "Accursed be the soil because of you. With suffering shall you get your food from it every day of your life.... With sweat on your brow shall you eat your bread..." (Gen. 3:17–19). The children have grown up in a single moment and know what they have done. Their punishment is the very thing they thought they wanted — to be alone with themselves.

The author of Genesis is not concerned to describe just what Adam and Eve did in their sinning against God. The story simply describes the cause and the effect — out of self-love, human beings ran away from intimacy with their loving Father and became parents to themselves. The disobedient children engendered the adults. The pages of the Old Testament, filled with Towers of Babel, harlotries of the heart, violence between brother and brother, nation and nation, dramatically cry out to us that this is our story also. Adam and Eve's sin is ours and our figleaf-excuses no different from theirs.

We live in a false world that we continually create within ourselves and show on the movie screen of our own minds. No one except us comes to this interior theater, but we hardly notice, so in love are we with our own false image and its creator, ourselves. In every movie we play the hero, refusing to see that we are also the villain. We fear God's terrifying punishment, God's self-revelation as utterly different from our poor selves, and so we hide, not as Adam and Eve hid behind fig leaves in their nakedness, but behind the masks and games that separate us from God, from our once-honest child-selves, and from the world around us. Like all pathological liars, in the end we come to believe our own lies. In our "splendid isolation" we tell the world we are happy and healthy, even as we drink, drug, and eat ourselves to death. We desperately seek to be loved by others rather than to love them, and we try to take their love by force. We destroy the very love we crave in the depths of our being while our false selves feed on the flesh and bone of our brothers and sisters.

If we kill our brothers and sisters, they cannot love us, and without their love we cannot live. We must let our false selves die so that our brothers and sisters may live, and we with them. Yet we seek to place the blame on others for our misery, as poor Adam tried to convince the God of truth that he was no sinner: "It was the woman you put with me; she gave me the fruit and I ate it" (Gen. 3:12). The hand that kills us is our own, as the hand that took the fruit was Adam's, but we refuse to accept the truth that we ourselves cause our unhappiness. It is no wonder that God pitied and loved us broken, blinded children enough to die at our hands so that we might see God and live.

St. Paul, who held the coats of the men who stoned a martyr, accepted his guilt because he first had the courage to face his loneliness. Blinded and helpless at the sight of himself as he was, Paul confessed,

> . . . but I am unspiritual; I have been sold as a slave to sin. I cannot understand my own behavior. I fail to carry out the things I want to do, and I find myself doing the very things I hate. . . . The fact is, I know

of nothing good living in me — living, that is, in my
unspiritual self — for though the will to do what is
good is in me, the performance is not, with the result
that instead of doing the good things I want to do,
I carry out the sinful things I do not want. When I
act against my will, then, it is not my true self doing
it, but sin which lives in me.... In my inmost self I
dearly love God's Law, but I can see that my body
follows a different law that battles against the law
which my reason dictates. This is what makes me
a prisoner of that law of sin which lives inside my
body. What a wretched man I am! Who will rescue
me from this body doomed to death? Thanks be to
God through Jesus Christ our Lord! [Rom. 7:14–24]

In a truthfulness that shattered his false god and false,
role-playing self, Paul found out who he really was. We
too in moments of crisis in our lives catch a glimpse of our
brokenness and a vision from God's revealed Word of what
we could be. If we continue to live in the tearing tension
of fear and guilt, our anxiety will only grow. We must rise
from eating husks like swine (Luke 15), return to our true
home, and be reconciled again with our heavenly Father,
whose hands are filled with the Bread of Life.

God's revelation leads us toward a true understanding
of our real and our false selves. In the first book of the
Bible, God goes about creation not as an "I" but as a "we."
And so we were created in the image of community, three
Persons loving as one, who freely wished to share their
love and their life with us. God said, "Let us make man
in our own image, in the likeness of ourselves..." (Gen.
1:26). We are made out of God's infinite love in order to

be loved and to love. God, who is love by nature (1 John 4:8), creates us in order that we might join with each other and with God, sharing in the ecstatic happiness of God's self-giving. In such self-emptying love for the other, each person is born into true identity that bends us toward each other as naturally as flowers toward the sun.

St. Paul captures the noble calling that God gives to us human beings:

Before the world was made, He chose us, chose us in
   Christ,
to be holy and spotless, and to live through love in
   his presence,
determining that we should become His adopted sons,
through Jesus Christ
for his own kind purposes,
to make us praise the glory of his grace,
his free gift to us in the Beloved
in whom, through his blood, we gain our freedom,
the forgiveness of our sins.
Such is the richness of the grace
which he has showered on us
in all wisdom and insight.

[Eph. 1:4–8]

As Paul was all too aware, however, we are not now, strictly speaking, the images of God. Only Jesus Christ, the pre-existent Word of God from all eternity, is perfectly "the image of the invisible God" (Col. 1:15). We ourselves are made according to the Logos, the Word in whom all things are made (John 1:3; Col. 1:16), and carry in our deepest selves the shape of God, as Mary bore the infant Christ. He is not us, but we share with him a family likeness. Never can we lose our resemblance to God. It consists of the potential locked deeply within each of us. But like Christ's grain of wheat, unless the shell be broken and the dynamic potential be freed to burst into abundant, new life (John 12:24), this very godly potential, nagging at our egos like a loving mother at a shiftless son, becomes the source of our greatest frustrations and fears.

Our bodies and souls are meant to be joined into a likeness of God's incarnate Word, Jesus Christ. Instead, from the first moment of our existence, we create a false ego that is less an image of Jesus than an image of sin and death. God's Spirit of love is not allowed to operate as the guiding force in our lives.

In our first, physical birth, we do not possess a *likeness* to Jesus Christ. Only the Spirit of the risen Lord awakens our conscious life in Christ. From non-existence, we enter the state of *being congruent* with our true self, like a larva filling its chrysalis with wet, curled wings. We bring the potential of our real, secret self to life when God is born in us from moment to moment, each morning of our life a Bethlehem, each night a crucifixion in which we die to our false self. With Christ we rise again in the newness of life, to love and serve.

We are our unique, true selves when we realize that we are children of God, sons or daughters of the Most High, and brothers or sisters of the only begotten Son of God, Jesus Christ. Paul writes: "... and you too have been stamped with the Promise, the pledge of our inheritance which brings freedom for those whom God has taken for his own, to make his glory praised" (Eph. 1:13–14). Through a constant conversion, or change of heart, we can become new by the love of God. That love is poured out into our hearts by the Holy Spirit (Rom. 5:5). We pass over from darkness into light, from our false ego to our true self, from our aloneness to a oneness with Christ. As the seed roots and grows into the tree of life, so in the darkness of our anxious fear we send out limbs that twine with the arms of God around the world.

At creation, the Trinity wrapped itself in love around our mother the cosmos and filled her with the seed of God. The child of that marriage of God and matter was Christ the Lord. With him in the joy of conversion we dance face to face, so close we breathe the same air, the Holy Spirit. In this shared life, God experiences our uniqueness as we experience God's divinity, finding our true selves by looking into God's face. With Paul we too can say, "There is only one Christ: he is everything and he is in everything" (Col. 3:11).

EXERCISE

Meditation on Breath

"And the Lord God formed man of the dust of the ground and breathed into his nostrils the breath of life and man became a living soul."

In the beginning, God gave human beings life with God's own breath. God still does. Without breathing, we cannot live. Breath is the bridge between our body, our spirit, and God. Yet how often do we take breath for granted?

Why don't we breathe deeply and rhythmically as infants do before they were taught how to be grown-ups? What changed us? In one simple word — fear. As we learned what we must and must not do, our chests and throats tightened, our backs and shoulders became stiff. Now that we know how to behave ourselves, at least most of the time, we should be able to "breathe easy" again, but the body hasn't yet got the message. It's still waiting for a blow, a disapproving word, a denial of love. You can now let your body know it's all right to breathe. Go ahead. Let your body know.

Close your eyes and breathe a few times with your total attention, tasting and smelling the air like a good meal.

Sit straight, inhale very slowly and deeply, hold the breath for just a moment, then exhale very gently, letting the air out equally from your nose and mouth. Let your chest expand, your shoulders relax. As you inhale, focus on breathing warmth up into the middle of your forehead, between your eyes. Exhale, sending waves of warmth down into your torso, your arms, your legs.

With your mind, follow the air down into your body, as it circulates through your abdomen, your legs, your arms, and notice if a warmth or tingling occurs as you trace your breath deep into every part of your body. Let your body lighten and disappear from your notice as you concentrate only on the air coursing through every limb, blood vessel, and cell. For this moment, you are nothing but the air you breathe, like Adam living only on the breath of God.

To help you create a smooth, even pattern of breath, to remind you where your breath comes from and where it goes, you can practice the Trinity breath-prayer. As you inhale, say to yourself, "Father," hold for a moment, saying, "Son," then exhale, saying, "and Holy Spirit." Do this several times until you no longer have to think or work at it.

Take in the whole creation and its Creator with the word "Father," feeling your body swell out, full of wind, earth, and sea. For the moment that you say the word "Son," feel the fullness of all creation, the breath of the ocean, rising and falling on the shore, the swinging of planets around the sun, the spreading of galaxies like circles around a rock dropped in water, all of this made flesh in the Son of God. As you exhale, saying "Holy Spirit," breathe out all you are, emptying yourself into the world like rain out of a full cloud, like ripe fruit falling from a tree, like the sun pouring out warmth, feeding the earth as a mother, flowing with milk, feeds her child. Experience the taking in of love, the fullness of love, and the pouring out of this love on the world, breathing slowly as if breathing were all you had to do or would ever have to do.

Now concentrate for a few moments on an icon, a crucifix, or holy picture, blinking when necessary, breathing deeply and regularly, with total awareness of the breath coursing through your body. Take in every quality of the object — its shape, texture, color. Close your eyes, cover them gently but firmly with your palms for two minutes, and concentrate on the image of this object in your mind, recreating every part of it as you breathe in and out, deeply and smoothly. Do not allow your attention to wander from your breathing and from the image you are holding in your mind. Now let both of them go, keep your mind quiet for a moment, and check your breathing again. Is your whole body involved in the act of taking a breath? Or has your concentration on the object made you forget to breathe? If so, go back and try again to keep up the deep breathing effortlessly, while you allow the image to settle in your mind.

Practice this exercise throughout today and the following days, keeping your regular deep breath going as you do other things, whether contemplating an icon or weeding the yard. Whenever you notice that your breath stops or becomes irregular as you go about your day's work, return to the Trinity breath-prayer: inhale, saying to yourself, "Father," hold for a moment, saying, "Son," and exhale, saying, "and Holy Spirit." Let the prayer become your breath and your breath become your prayer.

Notes

1. Gabriel Marcel, "L'existence et la liberté humaine chez J. P. Sartre," cited by Paul Tournier, *The Whole Person in a Broken World,* trans. John and Hellen Doberstein (New York: Harper & Row, 1964), p. 4.

— II —

In God There Is No Darkness

Have you ever wondered what our present world would now be like if God had *not* so loved this world as to have given us his only begotten Son, Jesus Christ (John 3:16)? All too often we miss the purpose of the enfleshment among us of God's divine Word. We believe God's Word in Jesus Christ came among us to die on the cross and in some legalistic, mechanical way we are automatically "saved."

Jesus Christ is "the Way, the Truth, and the Life" (John 14:6) that leads us out of darkness into light and makes it possible for us to become children of God, all who believe in the name of him who was born of God (John 1:12–13). The mission of Jesus is not only to reveal to us that the Trinity of a loving Father, Son, and Spirit is at the heart of all reality. He also makes it possible through the release of his Spirit for us to grow in the experience of the indwelling Trinity. We can know with absolute certitude that God loves us in Jesus through the Spirit. The sin and death experienced by our false ego can be conquered by our intimate experience of God's love for us. Guilt, fears, and anxieties can be totally eradicated from our hearts and we can live a new life in Christ.

Our faith given us through the Spirit of the risen Jesus shows us that God is a community of loving persons in whom there can be no false ego. "God is love" means that by the very one nature shared by the three divine persons, Father, Son, and Holy Spirit, each person in an ecstasy of self-giving passes beyond the limitations of an isolated self to risk self-emptying love for the other. Jesus revealed to us a Father who poured the fullness of divinity into his Son (Col. 2:9). Not only does the Son discover his being in the Father's love, but the Father mutually discovers his being in the Son's return of love to him.

In God there can be no false ego between two divine persons bound in ecstatic love. There are no defenses, walls, or barriers put up to protect the false self. There are no attacks against the others. There is only love. That love is the intimacy of self-giving and self-discovery in the self-giving. Love truly differentiates as it unites.

Such knowledge of the Trinity would be ineffectual unless Jesus made it possible through the outpouring of his Holy Spirit that we might experience this dynamic self-giving love of Father, Son, and Holy Spirit going on at all times within our very beings. Our bodies are truly temples of God since the Holy Spirit dwells within us (1 Cor. 3:16; 6:19).

Our Christian faith convinces us that the ecstatic love of the Trinity explodes out through the same Spirit of love as self-emptying love toward a created world. St. Irenaeus of the second century describes human beings as "empty receptacles" to be filled by God's goodness.

If God is love, God must be self-giving, for that is what

love is. But if God is self-giving, God must be an involving God who wants to get closer to us, not merely by giving us material gifts of creation, but ultimately God must want to share divine personhood with us. God wishes not just to communicate ideas about divinity to us, but to be in intimate *communion,* ecstatic union, with each of us.

God's loving movements at all times are invading, bombarding, penetrating us at the deepest levels of our being. These are called by the early Fathers "God's uncreated energies of love." These are God as differentiated Father, Son, and Spirit, giving themselves in the unique self-gifting of Father, Son, and Spirit. Such uncreated energies are found as God counts the very hairs on our heads (Luke 12:7) and takes care of all our needs. They are found especially in God's self-giving to us person-to-person in prayer and in the Eucharist, but also when we love one another with God's very love in us that becomes perfected in our human love (1 John 4:12).

The good news that Jesus came to reveal to us and make possible through his Spirit is that the Kingdom of God, the indwelling Trinity, is truly within us. We can come to know and love God and are known and loved by God as God's children, as a part of God's unique and only-begotten Son. The doctrine of the Trinity becomes for us now a living experience of the one and united God, essentially love, and always in the same relationship to us but now manifested to us in divine energies meeting us at each moment.

Christ came as the light into a world of darkness but the darkness did not comprehend him (John 1:4–5). More than this. The darkness in the hearts of many around him rose up and snuffed out that divine Light. He preached the "good news" that God is a loving Father of infinite mercy, forgiving all people their sins, bringing healing love to the lonely and desolate, hope to the hopeless, freeing all from fears and worries. This man who stood before his listeners was claiming that he was the focal point of the presence of God's dynamic power, bringing about new, life-giving relationships directly with God.

Jesus calls us to overhaul completely the habitual values by which we live when we are under darkness and guided by a self-seeking ego. Like children, we are to become totally dependent upon God's Spirit for this knowledge that is beyond our own power, infected as it is by our false ego:

> I tell you solemnly, unless you change and become like little children you will never enter the kingdom of heaven. And so, the one who makes himself as little as this little child is the greatest in the kingdom of heaven. [Matt. 18:3–4]

We have seen the great dignity to which we have been called by God's free choice, namely, to enter into the intimacy of God's love and to become a totally new creation by God's uncreated energies working within our lives to make of us regenerated children, born of the Spirit from above (John 3:3–5). We have also seen the negativities in our lives that hold us back from realizing our true selves in a growing oneness with Christ. Let us focus in more detail upon the false ego that sin has brought into existence. Before we can move to our true selves in Christ, it is necessary to see who we now are in our illusory selves.

EXERCISE

Experiencing the Divine Paradox

Look around you. Become aware of what you taste, smell, hear, and see. Scan your body and be aware of how what you sense affects your emotions, your way of holding the body, your sense of well-being and relaxation or tension. Take in your impressions as you inhale, forget them as you exhale.

How many items, roughly, are you aware of? Include the data of all the senses and of your feelings. Understand with your body and your feelings what "many" means. Be aware of the impact on you of each person, happening, and object in the room.

Now close your eyes, turn your attention inward, and hold still with both your mind and body. One by one, let the things you sense drop away, as they did when you exhaled them gently, until your mind is empty. First, forget what you smell, then what you hear, then what you see. Concentrate on your breath going in and out, and then focus your attention on the moment when the breath is between going in and out. Keep your awareness there, hold your mind still, and let no thoughts into your mind for a few moments. Forget everything in the room or in your body for these few moments. Say to yourself as you stop between breaths, "One." Say it again, and keep your mind on "One."

Next, consider how different you felt when you received many impressions and when you received just one. Ask yourself, which is truly the world around me? Is the world many or one? Is it both at the same time? If it is easier to feel the world as many than it is to feel the world as one, ask yourself why that might be true.

In your own consciousness, all your separate experiences exist. They become one experience through God, whose love gives them common ground and who is at once One and Three. We know God simultaneously as both ourselves and other, as both immanent and transcendent, incarnate and pure spirit.

— III —

The Strategy of the Ego

Our self-centeredness and pride cause us to lie to ourselves in order to escape from guilt. We don't want to take responsibility for our brokenness, so we attribute all our temptations to the Devil or even to God. In doing so, we totally ignore the true nature of God and our own human nature, as St. James clearly teaches:

> Never, when you have been tempted, say, "God sent the temptation"; God cannot be tempted to do anything wrong, and he does not tempt anybody. Everyone who is tempted is attracted and seduced by his own wrong desire. Then the desire conceives and gives birth to sin, and when sin is fully grown, it too has a child, and the child is death. [James 1:13–15]

We need instead to present ourselves to God as who we really are, shaped by heredity, education, the action and reaction of others upon us and ours upon them. Being honest with ourselves and with God means tracing our fear and guilt to their source: a false self that we created to replace the image of God. Our Christian spirituality

36

must rest upon an understanding of the way the false ego works as well as on the power of God's indwelling love to transform this illusory self into our true self.

We are dominated more by fear than by love. We find ourselves being unloving almost universally toward those who dislike us and even from time to time toward those whom we profess to love, such as husband, wife, children, and friends. Perhaps they will know our lack of love, so we reason, and cease to love us. Perhaps they will even do us harm. And so we create fear, the fear Jesus said only perfect love can cast out.

It is the state of fear from which we must be delivered, for the objects that we fear are often only in our minds. The nation's number one health problem is not bodily disease but rather emotional and mental illness. And most of these psychic disturbances are due to needless fear. Many doctors are concerned with healing the effects of fear. But if we are to attain wholeness of body, soul, and spirit, we must discover the root of fear, which is a lack of trust in God's loving care for us.

As Christians we have heard from Scriptures that God is loving, cares for us at all times, in all circumstances, and that we have no need to be anxious about anything. But still we generate new fears. One author describes how fear spawns new fears and such fears are passed on to others:

> We are afraid we shall not succeed in business, and we create our own failures. We are afraid we shall not have the money to pay our bills for the current month and we generally lack something because we have created that lack. We fear bad luck, disaster and death, and it is a wonder that man has not swept

himself off the face of the earth through his fearful creations.[1]

The story of Adam and Eve in the garden of Eden is our story, too. We have inherited a primal fear of God that is spawned out of a primal guilt at having "offended" God, as if God had the ego's capacity for spite. This guilt exists in what Jung called our collective unconscious. We are tied to every sin of those who have preceded us. Being born human already preconditions us to live in fear and guilt that block our sharing of God's life. This primal fear that we have disobeyed God and are guilty of divine wrath and punishment promotes fears within us. We fear God whom we should in fact love. We accept a false perception of God as a vengeful, punishing Jehovah, and like Adam and Eve we want to avoid God's accusing eye.

We accept the ego's claims that we are unworthy to be loved by God or anyone else. But the ego in its pride has us deny any guilt. The guilt for all our fears and lack of love has to be projected outside upon others. We accept the principle of cause and effect, but the ego twists and reverses just who is the true cause and what is the effect.

The ego completely convinces us that we are not the cause that creates a world separate from ourselves as its effect. "If only" becomes our acceptance of the ego's persuasion that the cause of all our fears and guilt is really in someone other than ourselves. If only that other person were not so greedy, I would be more generous, we say. Like King David, embarrassed at his adultery, we squirm and refuse to hear the prophetic word being sounded in the depths of our being: "Thou art the man!"

The more we yield to the ego's strategy, the more powerful the ego becomes. Our true self becomes suffocated deep down within us. Fears and guilt mount as the false ego becomes more dominant. The gap that separates us from our true self widens into an abyss. We run further "east of Eden" (Gen. 4:16) as Cain separated himself from his family and from God after having slain his brother. Higher walls and protective barriers are built up around our ego, which attacks others or withdraws into lonely isolation.

Our deepest longing is for true love from God and neighbor. Yet the enemy that prevents it lies within us. Our ego holds the key to the door that would allow us to pass humbly and gently out into the loving arms of God and others. And so day after day, year after year, we remain locked into the illusory self that creates illusory, separated worlds of enemies outside of us.

Our self-centeredness resorts to aggression and attack to retain the world it has created, a world that says we can exist independently of all others. In the words of the lawyer in Albert Camus's *The Fall,* we can say to ourselves:

> Fortunately I arrived! I am the end and the beginning; I announce the law. In short, I am a judgepenitent.... Ah, *mon ami,* do you know what the solitary creature is like as he wanders in big cities?[2]

Is there a way out? Can no one come to our rescue? Are we destined to remain locked forever inside, tormented by the false ego? Such a need expressed from the depths of our heart becomes like a ray of light shining through the cracked wall of our inner prison. It can lead us out if only we want to leave through the veil of the temple, ripped open by the self-sacrifice of Christ on the cross.

Please Hear What I Am Not Saying

Don't be fooled by me.

Don't be fooled by the face I wear.

For I wear a thousand masks, masks that I'm afraid
to take off.

And none of them me.

Pretending is an art that's second nature with me,
but don't be fooled.

For God's sake don't be fooled.

· · · · · · · · · · ·

Only you can call me into aliveness.

Each time you're kind, and gentle, and encouraging,

Each time you try to understand because you really
care, my heart begins to grow

Very small wings, very feeble wings, but wings.

With your sensitivity and sympathy, and your power
of understanding,

You can breathe life into me.

I want you to know that.

I want you to know how important you are to me.

How you can be the creator of the person that is me
if you choose to.

Please choose to.

You alone can break down the wall behind which I
tremble.

You alone can remove my mask.

You alone can release me from my shadow-world of
panic and uncertainty,

From my lonely person.

Do not pass me by. Please. . . . Do not pass me by.

· · · · · · · · · · · · ·

Who am I, you may wonder. I am someone you know
very well.
For I am every man you meet and I am every woman
you meet.

— Anonymous

EXERCISE

Healing the Pain of Separation

Sit with your eyes closed, relaxing your body head to toe,
part by part, breathing deeply. Look back at your recent
life until you remember a time when someone close to you
got something you would have liked for yourself. It could
be a raise, a husband, or a new car. Think back on how you
felt when you were jealous. Let the feeling come over you
again, recalling all sounds and images from the occasion.

Now return in your mind to the situation that made
you suffer this pain, this sickness. Be aware that just as
you *chose* to feel this pain, you can choose not to have it by
seeing the other person as part of the same body, part of
you, like your own loved child, mother, husband. Remember the last time you gave a gift to the person you most
love. See again the room you were in; recreate the sounds
and images from that moment. See his or her face smiling,
relaxing in pleasure; feel the loved person's lightness and
joy in receiving something good from you, through you.

Visualize your body as a sinuous, vitally alive, growing vine, with branches unrolling from every inch of you,
bursting into flowers at your fingertips, tendrils curling
gently around the limbs of others, becoming part of them,
drawing life from them, giving life back to them. See the

living energy of Christ flowing into your whole body and out again into others, bringing forth the fruit of the Vine — love.

Breathe in, saying slowly with Jesus, "I am the Vine"; breathe out saying "You are the branches."

Notes

1. Cited by Jon Mundy from "Triton: The Magic of Space," pp. 138–149, in "On Fear," *Spiritual Frontiers,* no. 3, vol. 4 (Summer 1972), p. 171.

2. Albert Camus, *The Fall,* trans. Justin O'Brien (New York: Vintage Books, Random House, 1956), p. 118.

— IV —

Turning Around

Father Henri Nouwen spent several months living among the Third World poor in South America. He writes in his diary:

> Sometimes I see humanity as a sea of people starving for affection, tenderness, care, love, acceptance, forgiveness and gentleness. Because they receive so little if anything of it at all, they make pistols, guns, rifles, missiles and similar toys instead of asking for attention.
>
> Everyone seems to cry: "Please love." The cry becomes louder and the response so inaudible that people kill each other and themselves in despair. The little orphans tell more than they know. If we don't love one another we kill one another. There's no middle road.[1]

As there is no middle road between love and death, there is none between life in light and life in darkness. Our true self, surrendered to God's will, lives in the light of God's love, while the false self, hanging on our own will like a bat in a cave, lives in darkness. From the pain and loss we all go through as we grow up, we learn that hatred hurts and love heals. Hatred separates us so that we can hurt each other without seeing that we hurt ourselves. Love puts us in the other person's skin; we do not hurt others because they are us. In knowing myself through you, in choosing to love you as myself, I am surprised by happiness.

Since we human beings can love by choice and in that love transcend our own small selves, we are *responsible* in a way that no other creatures on the face of the earth are responsible for what they do. Your dog thinks you're God, whether you're good or bad, and serves you, even killing at your word. But we are not imprisoned by such conditioning. We can think and will, having a mind that knows God is Absolute Meaning, and a desire that wants to stretch the body, mind, and spirit until they touch that meaning.

The call to repentance, this returning to our true self, is also a turning to God against whose perfect goodness we see our broken souls. We must begin our inward-turning with an honest look at our existential place in time, our being-in-the world as "thrown," as inauthentic,[2] broken, and incomplete, not responding to God's love because we don't want to. There it is. We would rather not know the love of God or know who we really are. We would rather watch a football game, or eat a pizza, or read the stock market report than know who we are. God calls to us and we cover our ears:

Listen, you heavens; earth, attend,
for Yahweh is speaking,

"I reared sons, I brought them up,
but you have rebelled against me...
A sinful nation, a people weighed down with guilt,
a breed of wrong-doers, perverted sons.
They have abandoned Yahweh,
despised the Holy One of Israel,
they have turned away from him....
Come now, let us talk this over,
says Yahweh.
Though your sins are like scarlet,
they shall be as white as snow;
though they are red as crimson,
they shall be like wool.
If you are willing to obey,
you shall eat the good things of the earth.
But if you persist in rebellion,
the sword shall eat you instead."
The mouth of Yahweh has spoken.

[Isa. 1:2–4, 18–20]

We are God's people, the sheep of God's pasture, and we
know God's voice, even when it breaks our hearts, convicts
us of self-worship, tells us to fall on our knees.

"But now, now — it is Yahweh who speaks —
come back to me with all your heart,
fasting, weeping, mourning."
Let your hearts be broken, not your garments torn,
turn to Yahweh your God again,
for he is all tenderness and compassion,
slow to anger, rich in graciousness,
and ready to relent.

[Joel 2:12–13]

God forgives us. That is the Good News. God puts himself in our hands, becoming the Way, the Truth and the Life (John 14:6). Here I am, God says. Here we are. Will you come, little children? Will you turn around? God says to us what Jesus said to the daughters of Jerusalem, and never stops saying it. God says we have reason to weep. "The time has come, and the Kingdom of God is close at hand" (Mark 1:15). Turn around, the Good News is in front of us. We only have to take the next step.

Where we were not, where only a false self jumped up and down like a demented marionette, there we suddenly are, ready for life, not death, eating the Bread of Life, promise-crammed with immortality. The grace of God falls upon the hard desert sand of our hearts, stirring the seeds planted there. We do not have to hide behind masks or compete for the non-existent room at the top. We do not have to be separated from others out of fear they will attack us. We can shed our dead skin and be ourselves, giving up our false shell to become the butterflies we were meant to be.[3]

When Jesus called us to share his eternal life, we responded according to our own ideas of what we wanted to hear. When they heard his words, the Romans washed their hands of him: the Zealots expected their messiah to overthrow the occupying Roman army. They were not prepared to turn away from violence to follow him whose only violence was against his own human weakness. The Good News that Jesus preached was that God is a loving and forgiving Father. God heals the lonely and desolate, bringing hope to the hopeless. To turn around and see God's face is not to be afraid, for God's perfect love casts out fear.

We cannot save ourselves, and we cannot go on living as if Christ had not told us we had to turn around and look him in the face (Eph. 2:8–10). Our lives are no longer our own. But now we know what we are, and how much we need a savior:

> In particular, I want to urge you in the name of the Lord, not to go on living the aimless kind of life that pagans live. Intellectually they are in the dark, and they are estranged from the life of God, without knowledge because they have shut their hearts to it. Their sense of right and wrong once dulled, they have abandoned themselves to sexuality and eagerly pursue a career of indecency of every kind. Now that is hardly the way you have learnt from Christ, unless you failed to hear him properly when you were taught what the truth is in Jesus. You must give up your old way of life; you must put aside your old self, which gets corrupted by following illusory desires. Your mind must be renewed by a spiritual revolution so that you can put on the new self that has been created in God's way, in the goodness and holiness of the truth. [Eph. 4:17–24]

When we look at what we are and what Christ is, our hearts break, we rend our garments. Any moment may bring us face to face with Christ — a serious illness that forces us to a long, lonely convalescence, a retreat, the death of a loved one, or economic ruin. Our false ego needs to be jolted out of its smug self-sufficiency. Either we drug ourselves like alcoholics into thinking that nothing is wrong with us, or con ourselves into thinking we can take care of our problem alone. "If we say we have no sin in us, we are deceiving ourselves and refusing to admit the truth; but if we acknowledge our sins, then God who is faithful and just will forgive us our sins and purify us from everything that is wrong" (1 John 1:8–10).

The Pharisee in the parable of Jesus stood before God in the front of the synagogue and found nothing wrong with himself or his conduct: "I thank you, God, that I am not grasping, unjust, adulterous like the rest of mankind, and particularly that I am not like this tax collector here. I fast twice a week; I pay tithes on all I get." The tax collector, however, was truly repentant as he cast his eyes downward within himself in his broken state and beat his breast, saying: "God, be merciful to me, a sinner." The acknowledged sinner, the publican, went home justified before God. "For everyone who exalts himself will be humbled, but the man who humbles himself will be exalted" (Luke 18:9–14).

Our greatest strength, as Mary Magdalene, the Good Thief, and St. Paul understood, is in our weakness.

> So I shall be very happy to make my weaknesses my special boast so that the power of Christ may stay over me, and that is why I am quite content with my weaknesses, and with insults, hardships, persecutions, and the agonies I go through for Christ's sake. For it is when I am weak that I am strong. [2 Cor. 12:9–10]

Before we can turn around, we have to look at our false face in the mirror and decide we don't want to be false anymore. But first we have to see how false we were, looking hard at ourselves in the light of what Christ is. Our weakness reminds us that we cannot save ourselves.

In our helpless weakness, we at last let go of our willfulness. At that moment of childlike trust, the risen, living Jesus Christ releases within our depths his Holy Spirit of love. We become uniquely and beautifully ourselves, set free from all fears and inner darkness by willing to live as the image of God.

As we decide to accept our ego's sinfulness and dereliction, we see we have been exiles in a foreign land. Our very broken condition is our means to rise and go back home to our heavenly Father.

Before the penitent St. Mary Magdalene could stand at the foot of the Cross with Jesus or meet him after he was risen, seven devils had first to be driven out of her. She did not have "innocence" to offer him, only a broken life and a broken heart. She became a "whole" and "holy" person, not in spite of her sinful past, but precisely in and through that brokenness that taught her to love much.

The story Jesus told about the prodigal son's return to his father illustrates how a fault can become a healing medicine. The virtuous elder son had never left the home of the father and consequently had never learned how much his father loved him. Our brokenness teaches us that we need God. St. Augustine writes that the decision to surrender all, even our sinfulness, to God's love, is rooted in trusting God's unconditional love.

> I am so sure of Thy love that I dare to come to Thee even with my unfaithfulness; Thou art able to love even my infidelity.[4]

No longer do we have to run away from God; we run *to* God.

We need more than a mere desire to return home to

our Father. Our acceptance of the sin and brokenness of our past and our turning toward God will not bring us permanently from darkness to light unless we courageously tear up the false self, moment-by-moment, as it tries to plant its roots back in our heart's soil:

> If anyone wants to be a follower of mine, let him re-nounce himself and take up his cross and follow me. For anyone who wants to save his life will lose it; but anyone who loses his life for my sake and for the sake of the gospel, will save it. [Mark 8:34; cf. Matt. 10:38; 16:24; Luke 9:23; 14:27]

Our new life in Christ must be backed up with denial of our false self, in every thought, word, and deed. Like the grain of wheat in the parable, we must be willing to die so that we may live and multiply.

Not only must we deny our false self, but we must positively put on Christ, ready to endure whatever suffering might come as we obey his word speaking within us. Christ does not ask us merely to suffer. He knows the false ego does not die without violence. A lifetime of selfish habits, rooted in fear and guilt, does not die easily. It requires no less than a crucifixion.

Are we ready to be converted to the Lord, to turn our faces to his face? Our cry is, "Come, Lord Jesus. Maranatha."

EXERCISE

Turning Your Life Around

Your body has been trained to act in ways that might at one time have been useful or necessary, but now limit your freedom. To begin dehabituating yourself, you might use several of the following techniques:

1. Folding your hands to pray. Try folding them in the usual way, then put the other index finger on top, lacing your fingers differently. Feel the strangeness of the new posture, and then switch back to the comfortable one. Keep moving back and forth between the two postures until both feel equally natural.

You have broken an ingrained pattern and taught yourself a lesson in freedom. Apply this exercise as often as you can to other conditioned forms of bodily behavior and enjoy the freedom this new choice gives you.

2. Now try a harder lesson. Choose one habit that really interferes with your growth. It may be abuse of cigarettes, food, or alcohol. It may be the desire to possess power, money, security, or a particular person. Be honest with yourself as you choose the habit you most need to break. Write it down briefly and look at it. Consider the form of behavior opposite to the actions your habit forces you into. Settle on one basic way that habit is expressed, whether it's opening the refrigerator door too often, or not coming home on time after work. Decide on what steps you will take to turn this habit around. Write the steps down, with a short prayer which you intend to say whenever the old, destructive habit turns up. As often as you have the

desire to be self-destructive, practice the new habit you
have chosen, with a new awareness that you are free to be
who you really are — the image of God.

Notes

1. Henri Nouwen in an excerpt from his diary in the *National
Catholic Reporter*, September 17, 1982, p. 7.

2. These are Heidegger's terms as used by Dr. John Macquarrie.
See *Studies in Christian Existentialism* (Philadelphia: Westminster,
1966), and *God-Talk: An Examination of the Language and Logic of
Theology* (New York: Harper & Row, 1967).

3. See Trina Paulis, *Hope for the Flowers* (New York: Paulist
Press, 1972).

4. St. Augustine, *Enarrationes in Psalmos,* 74, *PL* 35:953.

— V —

Receiving the Christ

Rejecting our inauthentic self does not mean that we have turned around to face both God and our real self, integrating them in a single act of pure love. We must become totally convinced by the working of the Holy Spirit that we are in desperate need of God.

We cannot heal ourselves, locked as we are in the small, dark room of our false self, with the door handle on the other side. Only the healing power of love can let us out into the bright light of God and our true self. But love is relationship. We reach out toward another who will touch and hold us, affirm us as worthy of being loved. Alone, I cannot drive away the desperate fear that I will be rejected as unlovable, for I know in my heart how broken and sad my false self is. A folk tale tells of a prince who was turned into a frog by a witch. A beast he must remain, until a virgin looks through him to his heart and loves him. We are that poor frog and Christ the virgin who loves and marries us as we are, thus birthing us into our true selves, branches of his Vine.

Yes, God loved the world so much
    that he gave his only Son
so that everyone who believes in him
may not be lost
but may have eternal life.
For God sent his Son into the world
not to condemn the world,
but so that through him the world might be saved.
                              [John 3:16–17]

Jesus Christ announced that heaven is already here, inside us, where God lives. As our false selves evaporate like fog in the sun, we see where we are: in the presence of God. God's love, concentrated in Jesus Christ, pierces through us until our false selves shrivel in its heat and our true selves unfurl like flowers in sunlight. As Jesus walked among the crowds, he loved, touched, and healed whomever he met. In seeing him, they saw the Father and knew that God was love, knew they were inseparable from God and from each other. Never did Jesus reject anyone, nor did he burden anyone with guilt. Instead, he lifted such burdens off our bent backs and took them on himself. His healings were a sign that a new world, a new creation, could be the home of all who made themselves one with him in love.

God overturns the values that guide men and women to choose what their false egos say they should choose. Money, power, aggression, and separation are to be replaced by the defenseless love of Jesus.

God chose, especially in the suffering and death of his Son, to confound the proud of this world, "For God's foolishness is wiser than human wisdom, and God's weakness is stronger than human strength" (1 Cor. 1:22–25). God's wisdom, so different from the wisdom of this world, flows out through the gently overwhelming Spirit of love. Within the Trinity, Father, Son, and Holy Spirit know that the true self has identity only when it loves in an emptying of itself.

Yet, we wonder, how can God love in this way, emptying himself, without ceasing to exist? Would we dare to surrender ourselves totally, risking all we are, if God had not first abandoned himself to crucifixion? Probably not. Most of us hang onto whatever we have, even if we are miserable in the possession of it.

If God's love had not reached out ecstatically through Jesus Christ, we would not have known how much God loved and wanted us; we would therefore have held onto all our dark doubts and ancestral fears. Because God sees us each as unique and worthy individuals, God gives birth to us again in a new life, mothering our true self.

We could not demand such love from God. Yet as though from some primeval knowledge, we hope for this unconditional love. In answer to our longing, God longed for us. God showed us the divine image, God's very self, in Jesus. When we see Jesus broken and emptied on the cross, we truly see the Father (John 14:9). Jesus mirrors God's love for us in his free gift of himself out of love. Hearing his words, we hear the voice of God, who promises to gather all men and women as healed children as they become one with Jesus in his gift of self.

Calvin Miller expresses the cost of God's love in his work *The Singer*. The troubadour who was killed comes back to life. He speaks to a young girl whom he had healed, and she in turn is moved to compassion by his scarred and wounded hands. She asks if they can be healed, and he responds:

> Earthmaker leaves the scars, for they preserve the memory of pain. He will leave my hands this way so men will not forget what it can cost to be a singer in a theatre of hate.... You will find, my child, that love rarely reaches out to save except it does it with a broken hand.[1]

Convinced that violence and separation breed more violence and separation, we cry out with Peter: "Lord! Save me!" (Matt. 14:31). By his love unto death, Jesus, whose name in Hebrew means "God who saves or heals," becomes our divine physician. It is by his human life lived in defenselessness and forgiving love that he becomes the Way for us to find our true self.

In prayer alone with God on the mountain tops or in the desert, as well as in his ministry of preaching and healing, Jesus learned how to let go of any temptation that would separate him from oneness with God as well as with all human beings. He loved everyone because he allowed the Spirit of God's love for him to make him aware of his Godhood. He had no false ego and so could love others without a thought of self. In every human encounter, Jesus entered, as we must enter, more and more into his true self, the self that was one with God.

The Pharisees and the Scribes could attack him verbally and members of the Sanhedrin could charge him with blasphemy, yet he would not return violence with violence (Matt. 27:13–14). Hanging between his heavenly Father and his suffering people, over whom he wept and whom he wanted tenderly to gather as a hen does her chicks (Matt.

23:38), Jesus could plead only for forgiveness as he died: "Father, forgive them, they do not know what they are doing" (Luke 23:34).

In choosing to die for humankind, Christ images the love of God for us all and at the same time passes over into a new existence, in mansions prepared for us also. God and humankind are one in the risen Jesus. By the Father's Spirit the humanity of Jesus reflects God's triune love for all human persons. Jesus is raised in glory and now has conquered sin and death, not only in his human-divine existence, but in ourselves, if we accept the good news and choose to live it.

Jesus Christ is the true Adam, the firstborn of a new race: the children of God (Col. 1:15, 18). He begets us into his triune family only if we are ready to deny our false ego and live according to that true self that accepts him. We have always been beautiful because God loves us unconditionally, but we have not seen ourselves: we're too busy to look in our mirror, Christ. When we pass over from darkness to light by experiencing Jesus' new presence in our lives, outpouring love as he did on the Cross, then the illusory self drowns and our true self awakens to new life in Jesus. Paul writes to Christians in Corinth:

> And for anyone who is in Christ, there is a new creation, the old creation has gone, and now the new one is here. It is all God's work. It was God who reconciled us to himself through Christ and gave us the work of handing on this reconciliation.... For our sake God made the sinless one into sin, so that in him we might become the goodness of God.
>
> [2 Cor. 5:17–21].

Jesus is still exhorting us, as he did those who heard his preaching, to wake up from our sleep and come out of our shadowy existence into the daylight of his healing love. He tells us to pay attention (Luke 17:3) and to pray always (Luke 22:46; 1 Thess. 5:17). Now is the precious, God-given moment in which we not only cry out for the coming of the messiah, but in which we accept him as a healer sent by God, who will raise us like Lazarus from the dead. Our desire for the Lord Jesus Christ to come and heal us and our acceptance of his love can come only from his Spirit. Alone, we are powerless to call him, even powerless to hear him when he calls us. Only the Holy Spirit can link us to him, joining the unknown God to us, joining mystery to matter, God to humankind.

We were made to be vessels of God, to carry in ourselves the love that holds the universe together, sustains it, and transforms it into God's image. The driving force in our lives, and in the life of every living thing, is to experience God's love and express it. Our lives have worth only to the extent that we pass God's love on to others.

As Christians, we believe that Jesus, true God and true man, promised to release in us God's Spirit of love. In that Spirit, whom Jesus could not give us until his death on the cross and his Ascension, we would be convinced of the truth he had taught by his life and his death.

And when he [the Spirit] comes,
he will show the world how wrong it was,
about sin, and about Judgment:
about sin:
proved by their refusal to believe in me;
about who was in the right:

proved by my going to the Father
and your seeing me no more;
about judgment:
proved by the prince of this world being already con-
    demned.
... But when the Spirit of truth comes
he will lead you to the complete truth,
since he will not be speaking as from himself
but will say only what he has learnt;
and he will tell you of the things to come.

[John 16:8–13]

The movement of the indwelling Spirit within us (Rom. 8:9) resurrects a nostalgia in the depths of our being for the home of our Father. The Holy Spirit gives us the courage to be discontented with our inauthentic self and to rise and go to our Father. We need only to ask the Father in the name of Jesus to pour his Spirit into our consciousness (Luke 11:9–13):

But you will seek Yahweh your God from there, and if you seek him with all your heart and with all your soul, you shall find him. In your distress, all that I have said will overtake you, but at the end of days you will return to Yahweh your God and listen to his voice. For Yahweh your God is a merciful God and will not desert or destroy you or forget the covenant he made on oath with your Fathers. [Deut. 4:29–31]

The voice of the Beloved within us crumbles our self-invented wall dividing us from the Father. The joy of being reconciled with us thrills the heart of the Father who had never left us, but lived silently in the tomb of our hearts waiting for resurrection. Our Father says: "We are going to have a feast, a celebration, because this son of mine was dead and has come back to life; he was lost and is found" (Luke 15:23–24).

Our separation from God and from our fellow human beings was a lie created by our false ego. The love of God shines through it like sunlight through stained glass.

All too often we have interpreted the atonement of Christ for our sins in static, legalistic terms. But the atonement is the Holy Spirit moving through our darkness on wings infinitely bright into our heart's core, once we are emptied of false ego and longing to be filled with Christ's love. The Spirit uncovers for us the good news — that we were always in God's loving plan as members of Christ.

> Before the world was made, he chose us, chose us in Christ, to be holy and spotless, and to live through love in his presence, determining that we should become his adopted sons, through Jesus Christ....
>
> [Eph. 1:4–5]

The Spirit first pours into our newly conscious hearts faith, hope, and love to comfort us in our exile.

> They had left in tears,
> I will comfort them as I lead them back;
> I will guide them to streams of water,
> by a smooth path where they will not stumble.
> For I am a father to Israel,
> and Ephraim is my first born son.
>
> [Jer. 31:9]

Our quaking fears and guilt are dissolved. We see that God has never left us and that God's merciful love is above all

God's works. In the experience of that love, in the now-moment, pouring into us from the fullness of the overflowing triune God, we live on love as God does. We wake up from the dark night of unreality to the daylight of God's everlasting love.

By leading us deeper and deeper in prayer, beyond words, which can often be manipulated by the false ego's desires, the Spirit prays within us, to the Father through the Son (Rom. 8:26–27). In such prayer we experience the true, forgiving love of Jesus, who in his Spirit adopts us as the children of God (1 John 3:1; Rom. 8:15; Gal. 4:6), heirs of heaven and co-heirs with Christ forever.

Through Christ's atonement, we understand by the Spirit our authentic beauty in God's healing love. No longer are we beasts driven by the autism of our false selves. We uproot all thought or action contrary to the teachings of Christ (2 Cor. 10:5) and become the beautiful image of God:

> I have been crucified with Christ, and I live now not with my own life but with the life of Christ who lives in me. The life I now live in this body I live in faith, faith in the Son of God who loved me and who sacrificed himself for my sake. [Gal. 2:19–20]

EXERCISE

Breaking the Old Vessel, Shaping the New

In Chapters IV and V we saw what it means to turn our life around, to open the door of our heart and let God enter. Now God is working within us from moment to moment. God will show us gently what to do and how to do it, and has forgiven us ahead of time for whatever mistakes we make. For years we have allowed self-centered habits to rule our body and mind, and these habits must be unlearned. The Holy Spirit, filling our vessel with love, begins to shift our desire to grab into a desire to give. How can we help in this work of transformation? We can *become* a constant, living prayer (1 Thess. 5:17).

Find a short prayer, ideally one of no more than seven syllables, that expresses your need for the forgiving love of Jesus. Keep the prayer hopeful, not self-condemning. Choose your prayer carefully and pray as you choose it, for it will be with you throughout every day. The use of a short phrase allows the prayer to be synchronized with your regular breathing pattern.

Practice saying your prayer as you breathe slowly and deeply, making it a part of your whole body, visualizing it flowing like air in your bloodstream, into every cell, keeping you alive and strong. Eventually this prayer will "say itself" in you, taking the place of a thousand clamoring worries, daydreams, and plans that now flood your mind, keeping it from being at rest in the presence of God. But at first you need to practice, noticing when you let your mind chatter or get carried away. Gently guide your mind back to the prayer, and be aware of God's energy pouring through you, relaxing and nourishing your body as the prayer focuses your attention on God's loving presence in you.

Putting this book aside, walk around the room, concentrating on your breathing, on your words, on your body's cooperation with the mind's directions. Practice dealing with any distraction that comes up, until the prayer comes naturally to your mind and lips.

Now try a harder exercise. Choose some simple, habitual occupation, such as typing a letter, peeling vegetables, or mowing the lawn. Practice adjusting the work to the rhythm of your breathing and the spirit of your prayer. Move deliberately, keeping your focus on this prayer that links your body, mind and spirit to the life of God that is in you and all around you. Each time you leave a distracting thought behind, each time you let your body move in harmony with the love that shapes the prayer on your lips, another tiny part of your brain in awakening to a new way of being in the world. An old habit is sawed through, like a rusty chain, and soon it will bind you no longer.

To help you remember to practice this prayer day in, day out, tape it to your tools, your desk, your refrigerator door. For best results, especially during the first week of the practice, allow some time daily for quiet activity such as walking alone outdoors, during which you can easily say your prayer, coordinating it with your breathing and your movements in a relaxed, slow rhythm. Enjoy the well-being that comes from perfect harmony with yourself, God-in-you, and the world through which God continuously gives himself to you.[2]

Notes

1. Calvin Miller, *The Singer* (Downers Grove, Ill.: Inter-Varsity Press, 1979), pp. 142–143.

2. For the technique of the breath-prayer as described here, we are indebted to Linda Sabbath, founder of the Thomas Merton Centre for Contemplative Prayer in Magog, Quebec.

— VI —

Being Forgiven

In his novel *Thérèse Desqueyroux,*[1] François Mauriac tells
the story of a woman driven by frustration and despair,
who makes an unsuccessful attempt on her husband's life.
Because he is only human, M. Desqueyroux cannot forgive
his wife and lift the burden of her guilt. She is condemned
to live out her life with him, hating as she is hated, mis-
understanding as she is misunderstood. All of us are like
Thérèse, though we may not go to the extreme of murder
in our loneliness and separation. We do not know ourselves and we are unknown to those around us. We too
are condemned to solitary confinement in the prison of
self.

When we stop running from God, hugging our false
ego, we see that we have been heading for the wrong goal,
and turn around. In the mirror of Christ we see ourselves
as we are, for the first time. The little murders in our past,
the deceit, the selfishness, that have separated us from others and from God disfigure our faces. To stare steadily at
ourselves without blinking, without turning away, takes

honesty and courage. Only because we are in love with God and God is with us are we able to bear the sight of ourselves, ugly as scars, beautiful as suns, animals on the way toward divinity. Because God knows us as the paradoxes we are — demonic angels, murderous lovers, lights under bushels — God dissolves our guilt in divine love. Unlike the miserable Thérèse Desqueyroux, we are loved because we are seen through, known fully, accepted unreservedly. God does not hate us for our plots against him; God does not condemn us for being broken on the rack of our false egos. What, then, does God do?

God dies as we must die, and rises transformed, holding us in both hands, close to his heart. No remote Sky God, this Father of ours, but an immerser of himself in created flesh and blood, planted in the soil of a woman's body, one forever with human beings. Unless Jesus had come to tell us, we would never have become aware that we were being lifted up in the arms of the Father, loved without knowing it, blind as newborn infants to their mother's face. Now that we know, we can open our eyes and see who it is that loves us, and love God back. The justice of God is not the justice of human beings. By dying to show us how much we were loved, Jesus showed us that to understand all is to forgive all. Nothing less than dying for us would have convinced us of God's forgiveness, God's parenthood, God's love. This love endures forever, in spite of what our egos have done, are now doing, will do in the future.

As the grain of wheat dies giving birth to the new plant, so Jesus died to bring the Father's loving Spirit to life in us, waking us from the deadly stupor of our false egos. We open our eyes like Lazarus walking out of the tomb straight into the arms of Christ, and see the light.

In the mirror of him, we see ourselves, transformed, reborn into new flesh, new blood, each cell recast into the image of God. The Holy Spirit speaks in us, true and strong as a heartbeat, drowning the tinkling cymbal of that liar, our false ego, which never gives up its attempt to murder God, the world, our true selves, so that it alone might live.

During his lifetime on earth, Jesus taught the love of God, lived it, healed the sick, pulled the drowning up by the hair. The crowds went wild, and didn't listen when Jesus told them it was harder to heal the soul than the body. "Unless you see miracles," he said sadly, "you will not believe." Like children at a circus, the crowds clapped their hands, wanting the next act. "Jump off the roof of the temple," the devil urged. "Be king," said the crowd. They didn't suggest that he suffer and die. That was his idea. We wouldn't have thought of it. Only God would think of such a thing.

When Jesus told us that we too would have to die to follow him into the arms of the Father, the crowds remembered that they had other things to do. The circus was over. "But all alike started to make excuses" (Luke 14:18). Even his chosen twelve disciples objected. A person suffers for being bad, they thought. Suffering is a punishment inflicted by an angry God. They did not yet understand that love is painful, and that the false ego dies hard. The sight of ourselves as we are in the light of God hurts and heals. To live you have to die, and dying hurts like birth. Only when the labor pains are over and the real self is born out of them, do we see who we really are.

Peter loved Jesus so much that he would have killed to protect him, but he couldn't stand *being* killed. When the crunch came, he said he had never known Christ. He ran away from the cross, leaving young John and a handful of faithful women to watch and weep. Such suffering, Peter thought, just might be contagious, and he wanted nothing to do with it. "Unless you suffer, you have no part in me," Jesus told him, but Peter wanted glory and power. Suffering was not what he had signed up for. In the garden, before Jesus was arrested, Peter took him aside.

"Heaven preserve you, Lord," he said, "this must not happen to you." But he turned and said to Peter, "Get behind me, Satan! You are an obstacle in my path, because the way you think is not God's way but man's." [Matt. 16:22–23]

Peter, like most of us, wouldn't take no for an answer. When the soldiers came to arrest Jesus, he lunged at one of them and cut off his ear. Then, of course, he ran away, for it is easier to kill than be killed, easier to hate than love, easier to project guilt than to own it as ours.

Yet Jesus went on saying to the end that the only way to follow him was to the death, into the open arms of the cross, burying who we think we are under a stone so we can become who we had never imagined.

Then Jesus said to his disciples, "If anyone wants to be a follower of mine, let him renounce himself and take up his cross and follow me. For anyone who wants to save his life will lose it; but anyone who loses his life for my sake will find it. What, then, will a man gain if he wins the whole world and ruins his life? Or what has a man to offer in exchange for his life?" [Matt. 16:24–26]

This saying was a hard one, and most people turned away from Jesus rather than hear it. Most of us do too.

Dietrich Bonhoeffer died in a Nazi concentration camp when he was thirty-nine, following Jesus into the black nowhere of a crematorium. He knew the difference between easy grace and the true cost of loving as God loves. He knew that only by giving up the illusion that he controlled his life could he follow his Master, go where his Master had gone, become who he really was. He had some sharp words for "otherworldly," disincarnated Christianity:

> We are other-worldly ever since we hit upon the devious trick of being religious, yes, even "Christian," at the expense of the earth. Other-worldliness affords a splendid environment in which to live. Whenever life begins to become oppressive and troublesome, a person just leaps into the air with a bold kick and soars relieved and unencumbered into so-called eternal fields. . . .
>
> However, Christ does not will or intend this weakness; instead, he makes man strong. He does not lead man in a religious flight from this world to other worlds beyond; rather, he gives him back to the earth as its loyal son.[2]

The earth with all its dirt and blood is where God chose to be born, raised to consciousness, and die. We and all the life of the planet beat with his heart, heal with his hands, share what he learned from wearing a body.

Jesus came to let us know how much God loves us (John 16:27), and words were not enough to speak for him. If parents love their children and do not want to see them hurt, how much more does God love us? God would rather suffer for us, his children, than allow us to bear pain.

But we cannot know the extent of God's love and suffering unless we share it. Forgetting our false selves, killing off our illusions, learning to love as ourselves what at first seemed other, always hurts, like the pain of childbirth. We feel the anguish, but we know it leads to life, not death. If the risk of death were not there, life would not be so dear.

Only the lover who gives up life for love can know how easy it is, how light is the yoke. If one is in love, there is no sacrifice. And so the old false ego dies, the real self stretches and wakes like a newborn child and is glad for the birth pangs. As our own cross becomes lighter, carried with love, we are paradoxically more in pain at the crosses of others. Especially heavy is the cross of their false egos, for we must see that the anger, the attacks, the rejection they hurl outward at us build walls that separate them from the love they need. In our ears are the words of Jesus:

> Love your enemies, do good to those who hate you, bless those who curse you, pray for those who treat you badly....

The only way to break down the walls their false egos have struggled to build is to see through them. As we feel their pain at separation from God and from us, we love them as ourselves, see them inseparable from us as our own faces. We do not merely imitate Christ, we become the skin of his hands as he reaches into the world to touch human beings. Is he wearing us or are we wearing him? No way for us to tell which, so close is the fit.

Since only our false egos would require a "program" or model to copy, we know that we are not "imitating Christ" as some outworn Western forms of spirituality would have it. Having known the living love of the Holy Spirit, how can we trade it for a sweet, painted plaster Jesus, created by human beings to teach us a sweet and painted piety? The Christ that burns at the heart of the universe teaches us not by rote but by a transforming experience of himself, which consumes the old ego, all that we thought was *us*.

When we enter into our innermost selves, we find both Christ and the real *us* tangled in an embrace so violent that it is hard to see where he leaves off and we begin. No mere pious imitation is going on here; no school child is parroting a teacher. A marriage of wills and hearts is being celebrated, out of which a new self is born. "Your mind must be renewed by a spiritual revolution so that you can put on the new self that has been created in God's way, in the goodness and holiness of the truth" (Eph. 4:23–24). This new self wants to obey God as the hand obeys the head, knowing that only in obedience will the false ego die, the new person live. Jesus reminded us that love is self-forgetfulness, learned by throwing away all that is not God in us:

> If you keep my commandments you will remain in my love, just as I have kept my Father's commandments and remain in his love. [John 15:9–10]

He longs to hold us close, but cannot if we disobey, shrivelling again into the deformed false self. Our body must shape itself to his, if we are to stand heart-to-heart with him, locked in that embrace that gives us life. Self-surrender to Jesus and the Father, who dwell within us, means that we obey moment-to-moment as God speaks the divine Word within us. As we enflesh our love by obedience to that Word, our ears and eyes open to the likeness of God in us that is our true being (Gen. 1:26). Our self is no longer the dwarfed false ego, but the image and likeness of God.

As Jesus turned inward to hear his Father's voice, he heard himself spoken into being, an echo of God, scarcely distinguishable from God. Because our true selves, other Christs by adoption, are made in the image and likeness of God, we too hear God utter us, if we hang on God's Word. God's Word issues in our acts, because both are shaped by one mind, God in us.

This never-ending day of Christ's indwelling presence lights us from inside, where no darkness is, because now this place is his. In its brilliance, you can easily distinguish truth from illusion. Simone Weil (d. 1943), the Jewish mystic drawn to Christianity, wrote of this new clarity of vision:

> We live in a world of unreality and dreams. To give up our imaginary position as the center, to renounce it, not only intellectually but in the imaginative part of our soul, that means to awaken to what is real and eternal, to see the true light and hear the true silence. A transformation then takes place at the very roots of our sensibility, in our immediate reception of sense impressions and psychological impressions. It is a transformation analogous to that which takes place in the dusk of evening on a road, where we suddenly discern as a tree what we had first seen as a stooping man, where we suddenly recognize as a rustling of leaves what we thought at first was whispering voices. We see the same colors, we share the same sounds, but not in the same way.[3]

Because we are new beings, we see a new world, not the poor, narrow one created in the image of our false egos, but the world as God made it. We become a body fit to be the Temple of the Holy Spirit, a skin fit to shape the bone and flesh of God.

Our shadowy side, our false ego, complains of the light and holds its ears against the voice of Christ. "Don't give me up," it clamors. "I will make you rich, powerful, admired. That other one, he will say you need nothing but him, he'll say to forget yourself, and love. He'll tell you to do his will, not yours, to give, not take. If you want my advice, you'll take everything you can get your hands on." Under this strident voice, we hear the gentle one of the indwelling Christ, saying, "Little children, love one another as I have loved you." That Spirit stirs in us like a child reaching for its mother, and draws our body, mind, and soul with it into a dance with God. Each step is in obedience, yet each step is where we want most to go. What God wants is for us to be more perfectly who we are, to drop those rags of ego that we still clutch over our naked true self, and to let all we thought was ours fall into the hands of others without having to be asked.

As Jesus dispossessed himself and even gave his mother away as he died on the Cross, shedding forgiveness like blood and water on us all, we too will let our ego die so that our real self can live. The love that we already share with Christ, we give away to others, having the more as we give, for love given away multiplies as did the loaves and fishes in the hands of Jesus.

The first attempt to walk in Christ's footsteps is to want to do what we think God wants us to do. In any given moment, we need to remind ourselves to do God's

will, not our own, and make a serious effort to know the
difference between the two. Should we fail, we acknowledge the failure, reaffirm the intention, and turn back to
Christ, again placing our feet where his walked. Each moment with him is the first. He is not concerned about suc-
cess. With him, no failure is so hopeless that it cannot be
transformed into its opposite. "My sacrifice is this broken
spirit, you will not scorn this crushed and broken heart"
(Ps. 51:17). Jesus is used to turning water into wine; it
was his first miracle. The more we abandon our old self,
moment by moment, throwing off the baggage of the ego
like a climber getting near the top of the mountain, the
more like Christ our true self becomes.

God shapes our every thought, word, and deed as we
listen with childlike openness and excitement and surrender to God's word. We peacefully and joyfully accept what
we are, the persons we meet, and whatever the present situation might be. We give up trying to figure out why we're
in this situation, how we can use it to our advantage, get
out of it, or lay it on somebody else. Instead, we give it
to God, along with ourselves, and follow where it leads,
abandoning ourselves like a dancer to the music. In fact,
we, the dancers, become the dance and the music, because
our old ego has been abandoned to both. Each moment,
each detail that we lay in God's hands makes us lighter,
freer. We surrender to God all the fears and anxieties of
the past, present, and future as we let God's energy pour
through us like rain into cracked ground, giving life.

As though we had been dead and entombed like Lazarus in darkness, we come totally to life in the complete
gift of ourselves to God, who gives us back to ourselves.
The wisdom of the Holy Spirit speaks in us with the words

of our own mouth, and we know good from evil, common sense from foolishness, peace from violence.

Jesus Christ is now our Lord, one with our deepest, truest self. "To me to live is Christ," we say with Paul, making God the subject and active verb of our whole being. Apart from him, nothing is, and we not only know this truth, we act it, live it, *are* it. In loving oneness with Jesus Christ, we find the Lord of the universe in whom alone we can live and move and be.

EXERCISE

Who Are You? You Are Forgiveness Itself

For this exercise you will need a mirror and a picture of the face of Christ that best represents all he is to you.

Begin by sitting with your back straight, your shoulders and neck relaxed, your hands palms-up on your knees. For at least five minutes breathe *consciously,* slowly and deeply, saying as you breathe in "To me to live..." and as you breathe out "...is Christ." Gently close your hands as you breathe in and open them again as you breathe out.

Take the words into your body with the air, lingering over "Christ," when you breathe his name out, as though you do not want to let it go, but have faith that he will be in you with the next breath. Breathe with the full attention that a newborn baby must exercise as it learns to use its lungs, not relying on the placenta of its mother for oxygen.

Concentrate on this rhythm of absorbing Christ into the living tissues of your body, feeling him rush with your blood into every cell, feeding and cleansing it, transforming its nucleic center into himself. Then feel yourself emptying out all you once were in a moment of self-forgetfulness, while you experience nothing but Christ-in-you, as you breathe his name.

Now set up the picture of Jesus in front of you, studying it carefully for at least five minutes, until every feature is as familiar to you as your own face. Continue to breathe as you did before, repeating, "To me to live is Christ." Let the face of Jesus soak into you like healing rain into parched ground, shape you like a potter's hands shaping wet clay, become *yours*. Close your eyes for a few minutes and bring back the face of Jesus into your mind's eye. If you need to refresh your memory, take a quick look at the picture before you, and close your eyes again.

When you are sure that you have made the picture part of you, open your eyes and look into the mirror at your own face. See it as it is, with all its freckles, warts, wrinkles, or scars. Then let this familiar old face go, let it die, not trying to hold onto it. As you breathe out "...is Christ," your hands opening, shutting your eyes if that helps you, see Christ's face where yours was. Breathe in again, closing your hands, and look at your own face, saying, "To me to live...." Breathe out "...is Christ," and see his face. Repeat this pattern until you can at will, easily and naturally, replace your own face with the face of Christ. As you do so, you may find one face merging with the other, so that you cannot separate them. Let that happen, being aware with St. Paul that "Now I live, yet not I, but Christ lives in me." You are no longer the person you once were, but have been forgiven by forgiveness itself.

Conclude the exercise by sitting for a few minutes with your eyes closed, *imaging* each of the people closest to you,

then seeing them as Christ. Resolve that during the next
day you will see his face and theirs as one, and that to help
this happen you will repeat your prayer, breathing slowly
in and out, "To me to live is Christ," as often as you can,
bringing to mind the face that is his, yours, and that of
every man, woman, and child God has created. You see
no fault in them because you are forgiveness itself. Your
love for them is Christ's own forgiving love of you.

Notes

1. François Mauriac, *Thérèse Desqueyroux* (Paris, 1927), cited by
Louis Vonden, S.J., *Sin, Liberty and Law* (New York: Sheed & Ward,
1965), p. 164.

2. Dietrich Bonhoeffer, "Thy Kingdom Come" (an essay written in 1932), in J. D. Godsey, *Preface to Bonhoeffer* (Philadelphia:
Fortress, 1965), pp. 28–29.

3. Cited in *The Fire and the Cloud: An Anthology of Catholic
Spirituality,* ed. David A. Fleming, S.M. (New York: Paulist Press,
1978), p. 318.

— VII —

The Grace of Sexuality

We have been created by God, out of God's infinite love, to
live, move, and have our being in God. Because we don't
know where we came from or where we're going, we prowl
about this earth seeking what we can devour, in a feverish
hunt for happiness. We look for it in money, possessions,
travel, food, sex, and yet all things fail to feed the hunger
in our hearts for a love that never ends, a happiness that
never stales.

From the first time we wept as infants left alone by
our mothers, we began learning that no one can be happy
without love. By ourselves we are helpless, threatened,
anxious — fragile as cut flowers. Without our roots deep
in the common soil, touching the roots of others, we dry up
and wither. Only by touching another do we know where
we leave off and the mystery of the other begins; only
by love can we penetrate that mystery. As babies raised
without the touch of love pine and die, so do adults if they
separate themselves from those who would love them and
be loved by them. Aborigines lying curled up together in

their cold caves perhaps understand more about our inborn
need of closeness than do we, separate, self-centered, and
lonely in our private bedrooms. The first loving touch of
another human being is the beginning of our discovery of
God, who is love (1 John 4:8), and points us toward the
center of ourselves where God lives. When we find God
there, we see that the other is waiting for us, because God
is at his or her center too.

The energy of God meets itself coming and going when
two of God's children meet heart to heart, eye to eye,
mouth to mouth, in an exchange of life and breath, close
as the Trinity itself, loving and being loved in an endless
circle of light and warmth, like the slow, timeless whirl of
galaxies spinning through each other in space. That love
that moved the sun and other stars precipitated the Word,
Jesus Christ. He was enfleshed as man so that we could
by knowing and loving him be gathered up in the arms of
God the Spirit, out of the swaddling clothes of our flesh.

God said, "It is not good for man to be alone. I will
make him a helpmate" (Gen. 2:18). God wants to give
himself to us in every possible way, first through Jesus,
who loved and touched his people with human heart, human hands, then through the Holy Spirit, who knits us all
into one seamless cloth that wraps the world, and finally
through the hands of another human being, laid on us in
love, as ours are laid on that other person. When we open
ourselves to this other person, we open ourselves to God
and God can touch us, like the sun touching the heart of
an unfurled flower. Closed, we can't be reached. But a life
spent loving is a life spent open. To reach out and receive,
we must open our hands; to be loved, we must first love.
The wife or husband next to you is more than your helper

on earth. He or she is your path to God, the tunnel at the end of which you see light. In the face of a wife laboring in birth or of a husband crushed at the loss of his job, you see the face of God, open to your love, wanting you to give it.

Deeper, deeper you go, till you touch the place in the other where God is, dropping your own veils of ego, self-defense, falseness as you go, until you both stand before each other and God naked as newborn babies. At this moment when you see God in each other, you see not only the image of Christ as he might have looked walking the earth, but also the pillar of fire, the plume of light that led the Israelites through the desert, the dance of all the tender, catfoot energies of God re-creating the world in, around, and through us. As the veils fall, we see God not through a glass darkly, but face to face in the light of love, in the one through whom God sees and touches us.

Each moment in which we give and take love, we touch God. When human hands meet in love, human bodies in desire to give and receive divine energies, God once again becomes embodied, incarnate, taking form as we give each other love. God knows who we are and what we need because God made us, and made us so that God and we could marry soul to body, spirit to flesh. We breathe *in* God's love, then breathe *out* love of this man, this woman, in whom God lives. Without God, we cannot love; without the other, we cannot show our love. In both, we forget ourselves to become ourselves: first becoming empty, that we can be filled to bursting, and at last become what filled us.

From the moment our father's sperm met our mother's ovum, both dancing expectant in the dark, knowing where to be, what to do, whom to become, we were human beings. But that silent embrace of our two halves as they made one male or female person was only the start of a long journey toward a distant point far past death, in the life to come. Each step of the way plants our feet deeper into the soil of earthly love, soil smelling rich as cowfields with the birth and life of bodies, the incubator of spirit, the mangers of divinity. In loving God we love God's world, we bend and kiss the earth that God has given us as home, as the temple of God's very self.

To understand what it means to love another human being as Jesus loved us (John 15:9), we must first understand the cost and reward of being human. In his *Christmas Oratorio*, W. H. Auden asks the Three Wise Men to explain what led them to Bethlehem. The first one says: "To discover how to be truthful now is the reason I follow this star." The second says: "To discover how to be living now is the reason I follow the star." The third says: "To discover how to be loving now is the reason I follow this star." And then, as if to sum up, they all say: "To discover how to be human is the reason we follow this star."

What does it mean to be human? Is it to be no more than an animal, a predator chief among predators, successful at satisfying needs for food, sex, and survival? Yes, one side of us is as simple and crude as the cat who pricks up its ears at the squeak of a mouse. Our most primitive brain, lodged in a lump at the top of the spinal cord, drives us to desire, need, take. Yet we differ from the animals in being stamped in the image of God (Gen. 1:26), a coining that makes us aware early in childhood of a world around us that is not ourselves, and later in life aware of our deep-running blood lines with the body of our race and planet.

The cat does not know it owns its paw until you step on it; if you step on another cat's paw, the first cat will look on with indifference, or even purr. How different the outrage of a child who sees her friend punished unjustly, and feels the hurt as her own, or out of love takes the punishment on herself.

Psalm 8 asks the question of God:

Ah, what is man that you should spare a thought for him, the son of man that you should care for him? Yet you have made him little less than a God.

[Ps. 8:4–5]

And so, despite our flaw — the failure to see and grow beyond the carapace of our own flesh, or embrace the other as ourselves — we are fundamentally more good than bad, because we are made God-like, to share the life of God. We know empty darkness only because we know the light of day; we know badness only because God has let us see the good in all creation (Gen. 1:31), including the good in ourselves.

For God has made us like God, able to love others as ourselves, enough even to lay down our lives for them. In our love for others we express the link between flesh and spirit, as God expressed it in the Incarnation. We cannot, short of committing the crime of suicide, dissolve into spirits, but must weave ourselves into the world's web, an embodied life entwined with other lives, weeping with those who weep, rejoicing with those who rejoice. We are one and many simultaneously, as God is One and Three. Like God, we are an intimate community of love, pouring ourselves out so that we may fill others and be filled. Dietrich Bonhoeffer wrote before his death at the hands of men incapable of love: "The Christian element is not something which lies beyond the human element; it requires to be in the midst of the human element."[1]

We have been saved and are being saved in this present moment, immersed in the human sea, bred and nourished by it as we once were by the waters of our mother's womb. As we grow up, so we grow *out,* taking our own, grown shape only to find that we fit a waiting gap in the cosmic Body of the Lord, like a sunstruck petal opening in the body of a rose. It was John Donne, the Christian poet, who expressed the oneness of all human persons in the body of Christ when he wrote: "No man is an island entire unto himself." He is more; he is part of the "continent." When a bell tolls to announce a death of another human being, we need not ask "...for whom it tolls," because it truly tolls for *me.*

Only because we cover our ears, not wanting to hear that we too die, only because we are afraid to wind ourselves into the swaddling clothes or the shroud of the other, do we remain deaf to the music of the human race's dance with God. Only by hiding from ourselves our true nature, which is to be love as God is love, can we fail in those intimate spaces of our lives where we express our love sexually. And we do fail often. Perhaps nowhere in our lives do we fail more in love than in this primordial act of sex that raises in us urges to possess, punish, and use, as well as to cherish and protect. This ambivalence has given sexual love a bad name; it is, for many, synonymous with the sin of Adam, to be feared and fled from.

Why are we afraid? Because we know that human love, in which God meant to encounter us through the embrace of creation, can be twisted into selfishness and even sadism. To know our need for human touch and love is not necessarily to fulfill it. Like a man trampling women and children to escape a burning building, the false ego tries to live by killing, not by loving, not by giving itself. Despite optimistic modern doctrines of progress and of innate human goodness, the most educated and materially blessed nations on earth have in our own time imprisoned, tortured, and incinerated millions of innocent people. Apparently, everything that rises does not converge.

The struggle between nations is only the struggle between persons, writ large. Peace at every level begins with love, and love is rooted in our sexuality. Being "in love" is, of course, the most celebrated of human experiences; for those brief weeks or months, the two lovers are aware only of being "we," not a separated "I." Long-term love between husband and wife costs more than romance: the ego is worn to soreness by chronic abrasion with another ego. But in love as in everything else, we get what we pay for. The more we try to love others, the more we open ourselves to both pain and joy.

Gregory Baum suggests that we find it hard to love because we find it hard to grow up.[2] As we have seen, growing up means "growing out," dropping our walls and opening in selfless love to another, *being* that other. We become a two-way channel through which the uncreated energies of God flow, perhaps to create new life, certainly to create a moment in which two are gathered together, becoming one, reliving that mystery at the dawn of human time when God breathed Spirit into dust and the first human beings became living souls.

What we feel about ourselves sexually, then, reveals what we really feel about our identity, about God, and about other human beings. Naked, we cannot lie about what we are. Carl Jung wrote that the sexual problems people brought him were invariably religious problems and religious problems always turned out to be sexual ones. Because God is love and gives himself to us as the incarnate Christ, we know God through flesh and spirit, then pour out through that same flesh and spirit the love we have been given, the love we now *are*. As God is married to the material world in the Incarnation, so we are married to our body and to the body of another. Our maleness or femaleness will color the expression of our love to other human beings and to God, as light is changed by shining through stained glass.

Our psyches are rooted in our "body-selves," which in turn are rooted in our sexuality. If we believe God looked on the bodies he created and called them good because they were made in the divine image, we should not find it hard to believe that God can share goodness with us through the goodness of another's body, and touch us through another's hands.

Sexuality is not opposed to divine love, but is a bodily celebration of it. To describe sexuality is to describe both love and what it is to be human. Our sexuality determines how we will choose to love others and be responsible for such choices. When we make love, we are no longer in our own hands, but have surrendered ourselves fully to another, and we in turn touch all that they are. The same uncreated energies of God that drive the nebulae to wrap starry arms around their centers and the same energies that spin the cells of our brains into thought, drive us through our sexuality into the dance of life with another human being. In that dance we move to the music of the other, hearing in their music the clapping of angels, the song of God.

Without growth into being man or woman, we do not grow at all. No saint ever lived who was not a real man or woman, glad for the loving touch of another. God made us to love, and we must love with all we are. In becoming totally human, totally incarnate, we become as much like God as we are capable of being, and as much ourselves. To be human is to be sexual, to become ourselves, to live genitally, emotionally, spiritually. To love with all we have is the only way to share all we have, to be all we can be.

Human beings have historically chosen one of three basic expressions of sexuality, depending on how much of themselves they have wanted to give.[3] The simplest, most primitive sexual expression is called "body-mysticism," as practiced, for instance, by the ancient Canaanites with their frenzied orgies and by the modern devotees of *Playboy*. Sexual pleasure makes body mystics feel powerful and real. To discharge sexual energy, to "have sex," is for body mystics a way of touching God. They have no idea who their partner is or might become and do not want to know. So little awareness has each of the other, they might as well be genitals meeting in mid-air. The false ego is the star of this purely genital performance, in which sex is power over a human being used as a "thing." Instead of becoming the other, exchanging glance of eye, heat of breath, and beat of heart, body mystics forget they are not alone. They go to sleep afterwards, or light a cigarette, or turn on the television. Above all, they feel sad, having nothing to do with themselves until the next coupling. Their lovers were wasted on them; they were having sex alone, sharing nothing.

Countering this infantile, self-centered sexuality is the asceticism favored by the civilized West in its dualistic adolescence. Reason is pitted against the body in a furious war. Religious philosophies based on the triumph of the sky-god over the earth-mother goddess exalt the "masculine" soul and express contempt for the "feminine" body. Only with the words of Christ did the world finally hear that contemplation is better than action, that there is no male or female in God. These words like so many of his other words were not heeded. Church leaders in the West went so far as to say that husbands and wives should make love to each other only out of desire to have a child. Hearing these words, ordinary men and women were stunned, afraid to laugh, ashamed to cry, yet knowing better than those who led them that they make love because they need to touch and be touched, to give and receive what they can from the bodies and hearts of their mates, made and given to them by a God who is love itself.

Many young people, and Christian moralists as well, have counter-reacted to dualistic asceticism. Sexuality to them is neither good nor bad, but neutral. They are neither ascetics nor body mystics, but endorse an attitude of "take it or leave it." Their sexuality is detached and cool. Men and women are no different from each other; sex is comic or boring and had best be gotten over with, like idealism or acne, in the process of becoming a sensible middle-class adult.

Common to all three approaches is the belief that human sexuality is something one *has*, not what one *is*, and that sexuality is outside the core of one's personhood. When God made us sexual beings, God determined that our sex, like all the other bodily functions, couldn't be turned off and on at will. Sex gives us more than pleasure; it reminds us that we are both body and soul and that God chose to enter that state with us. In the person we love and live with, we share who we are and who they are; we forget ourselves in becoming the other. Thus, sexual expression becomes a school for holiness, a way of knowing God.

The Old Testament Jews were holistic in their view of sexuality. God had created man and woman as total persons. The Old Testament word for intimacy is "knowing," which connotes a spiritual and intellectual experience, not merely a bodily one.

The whole person is a "bodied-being." Human beings are *enfleshed*. The Hebrew word for this state is *basar*, and the Greek word *soma* comes closest to translating it. Again, according to the Jewish mind, "body-ness" refers not to a piece of a person, but to the whole person. Thus human beings in their *flesh* can long for God (Ps. 63:1, 34:3).

Ruah is the Hebrew word used to express wind, or spirit-in-motion, indicating God's creative presence among us. Thus in the Old Testament, the body, or *flesh*, and the soul are one thing, not two.

In contrast to the Greco-Hellenistic culture that saw matter and sex as an evil illusion, the Bible considers a human being as a psychophysical unity. Body and soul, which God has joined together, are not to be split asunder, but brought into a harmonious whole through the Spirit. Man and woman are "ensouled" bodies and "embodied" souls.

The *Zohar*, a primary source for Jewish mystical wisdom, comments on the balance of body, mind, and spirit:

"These three grades (*nefesh, ruah, neshamah*) are harmoniously combined in those men who have the good fortune to render service to their Maker."[4] The *nefesh,* for the Kabbalists, is the bundle of primitive drives we now associate with the autonomic nervous system and the basic bodily functions it regulates. While these instincts must be guided, the Jewish mystical tradition does not find it healthy to repress them by harsh, ascetical practices. Asceticism is useful only to break destructive habits that could hinder spiritual development. Once such development is underway, the divine gifts of food, drink, and sexuality can be transformed into the sacred experiences they were meant to be. When Christ turned water into wine at a wedding, he was moving in just such a tradition as the *Zohar* later codified.

The *Zohar* makes explicit reference to the sacredness of sexuality, seeing it as a metaphor for the creative union of the Father and *"shekinah,"* or "Feminine Wisdom," another name for the *Sophia* of the Greek Christians. Husband and wife following the visionary Jewish tradition are to "focus as totally as possible on the (sexual) experience, so that it actually becomes a sacred form of meditation"[5] and re-enacts the cosmic dance between the creative opposites — positive and negative, masculine and feminine — uniting them so that their opposition becomes the very condition of their oneness.

Continuing the implicit incarnationalism of the Jewish tradition, the New Testament teaches the importance of the material body. As the human Christ was the visible aspect of God, the human body is the visible part of the one, indivisible, unique man or woman who we are. It was through his body that Jesus redeemed us, and it is through our bodies that we receive his body and blood in Holy Communion. If God himself made the body a partner of the spirit in his most intimate act of union with us, can we do less in our acts of union with one another?

Although St. Paul wrote to the Corinthians, "Your body, you know, is the Temple of the Holy Spirit" (1 Cor. 6:19), the dualistic influences of the Greeks largely prevailed in Christian teachings on sexuality, eclipsing the holism of the Old and New Testaments. In combatting the sexual permissiveness of certain heretics, early Fathers such as Jerome and Origen made an overkill in their antisexual attacks. St. Augustine, once a Manichean, set the tone for the separation of spirit and matter in his teaching on marriage, insisting that pleasure was allowable only as a reward for the pains that would follow procreation. Any indulgence in such a "secondary" end of marriage as pleasure without securing the "primary" end of procreation was sinful. In the same spirit, Origen went so far as to castrate himself so that he could not sin sexually. His violence was only a hint of what was to come in the battle against the flesh.

Sexuality is like an inflated balloon. Squeeze it at one point and it will swell at another. Angelism, to use Jacques Maritains's term, is the repression of our sexuality out of distrust for our sexual nature. To deny or ignore sexual energies is to invite them to explode into illness, compulsive behavior, or violence. The rapist, for example, wants not healthy sex but to hurt a woman. Sexual energies themselves are not at fault in such a case; the problem is in the mind that twists or represses them. Sin and sex are not to be equated in Christian teaching. The initial fall of humankind, which constitutes, in Paul's words, "sin in my members" (Rom. 7:23), was disobedience, not sex; it did not totally corrupt our human nature or our sexuality, though it made both susceptible to perversion.

We must avoid, on the other hand, any naive optimism that our human sexuality is perfect and that we can become perfect men and women through it. Our own personal experience bears witness that our love is not selfless like God's but twisted and stunted by our false egos. Not the body, then, but the mind is responsible for the failure to consecrate sexual energies. It is because of a brokenness in our minds that we make war instead of love.

In lonely suicides, broken marriages, and the abuse of children we see the results of our selfish failure to love one another as God has loved us. We like to believe we love those close to us, yet our actions often prove we love only ourselves. In the openness of the one who loves us, we ourselves are unmasked, and the sight is not pretty. Our weakness and selfishness must be faced; our fears and doubts admitted. The gifts we receive from the other demand from us sensitivity and good faith. We can give no less than we receive, open no less than we are opened to. Not self, but God in the loved one becomes our center. True love makes the awful demand on us to let the other be completely himself or herself. But what agony to let go of the other, to give up control!

Living for the other's true self is the way we find out who *we* are. We are as surprised at our discovery as the larva must be when it wakes to find itself a butterfly. To lock ourselves and our lover in the chrysalis of our selfish expectations is never to know the winged, many-colored mystery both of us might be. And so sexual love can and should be a chance to fly away and be at rest, to go where the Father is, into the heart of the human person who loves you as him or herself.

The sacred intimacy of sex is a sign that our call to oneness with the heart of Christ must be heard in the voices of our human friends and family. In commitment to another, we throw away all the dead weight of our false selves, to share nakedly who we really are, entrusting ourselves to another. Our need is to give as God gives, receiving nothing but the joy of the other, imposing no conditions and making no demands. Husbands, wives, are you loving each other in this way? Our passionate desire to receive the other's free gift of love is human *eros*, understandable only in relation to divine *agape*, its source and end. Only when we dance in the endless circle of love shared by the Trinity does our true self meet the true self of the other, both wearing the face of Christ and loving with his heart. As Jesus washed the feet of his friends, so we bend to serve the goodness growing in the one we love, pledged to guard it as a bird tends its nest or a shepherd his flock. And the more love we give, the more love grows in the place we have planted it.

Maurice Nedoncelle suggests that an accurate description of Christian love would include a synthesis of *eros* and *agape*. As sincere, passionate *eros* leads to loving union, *agape*, so sincere *agape* leads back to *eros*:

> There is an eros of an agape, a need to possess the spirit of dis-possession, a desire to find one's soul in losing it. Why should eros be only a will to monopolize and use? It is the desire of the best, and as such is destined not to use everything but to learn that it ought to serve the spirit of generosity.[6]

To give ourselves completely as a child opens his arms to his mother we have to be ready for anything. Like sexuality, love is tinged with newness and wonder at what will be in the "not-yet." We hope always that through love we will be taken where we cannot go by ourselves, into the land of milk and honey where we feed others and are fed.

True love never consumes the uniqueness of the persons who are joining themselves, but differentiates as it unites. As God draws us into the heart of the Trinity, we become at once more truly who we are and more truly God's. We become free to love in the same measure as we love, become ourselves in the same measure as we give ourselves away.

Love has everything to do with the ordinary events of daily living, since the giving of all we are and the receiving back of all we can be happens in the workshop, the nursery, the office. When we discover the energies of God in each other, we pour those energies into all we do, reconciling the world to the Father (2 Cor. 5:17–18). But the greatest creative act is a sexual one: the surrender of husband and wife to each other, the tumbling down of walls between their separate selves until they become one flesh and in a willing act of love pour out God's uncreated energies in the making of a child and the re-making of themselves as one flesh.

Desire for a child raises the mutual love of husband and wife to self-transcendence, in which they touch the generosity of God as Father, entering with God into the mysteries of creation, joining God before the world's beginning. Birth hurls parents into a dizzying surprise as they touch a new life, born of God's active love and theirs. Perhaps for the first time in their lives, they know God as a loving, involved God who is not far away, but the element in which they live, move, and have their being (Acts 17:28). They hold in their arms the creation of God as they themselves are held.

True love is to see others as God sees, knows, and touches them. To love truly is to see with the eyes of God, to go beneath the skin and plunge straight to the heart, where the other shows him or herself to be as unique as if alone in the world, the sparrow whose fall God notices, the lamb for whom Jesus died. True love is caring for the other, mindful only of the other's good. It is being quick to hear the other's need, to serve the other's growth toward his or her true self and carry the other into deeper touch with God. The prayer of Jesus before he underwent his death was that we would be one as he and the Father are one (John 17:21–23). Of this oneness, human sexual love gives us a glimpse, so that we see, however briefly, the light of God's love in the closing eyes of our lover.

EXERCISE

Giving Your Sexuality to God

First, practice your breathing exercises and your body prayer. Then, sitting with your face to the wall of your room, let your body relax, keeping your back straight, and breathe slowly, deeply, focusing your mind on your lower torso, the place out of which you might make new life. When you are ready to do so, tape a full-figured picture of Jesus on the wall at eye level and look steadily at it. Think of your own body as both male and female, for both are needed to bring new life into the world. Be aware of the currents flowing through your whole body, as they do when you make or want to make love. Sense the desire of God, flowing through you, to share all God is and to share all you are.[7]

Gathering together God's divine, uncreated energies, gently move them upward into your heart. See them flowing like rivers into a sea, pouring out new life. If you have trouble visualizing this outpouring, take a pen, draw a picture of a geyser, and tape it next to the picture of Christ. Look at it when you need help in drawing your own energies upward.

Notice the sensations of your body as you call forth all its powers, thanking God for the energies that keep you and all the race alive. Understand that you are not putting down your need to love, to give yourself, to spread your God-created powers, but that you are sharing those powers with the whole world.

Study the body of Jesus on the picture before you, and in your own mind. Draw his loving energies into every human being on earth, starting with yourself. Think of Christ's love as a geyser, an eruption within you. See it rise, pour out everywhere, carry you away in the flood.

Close your eyes, and for as long as you can, see this geyser rise from your feet, to your lower body, into your heart. If visualizing the geyser rising in you is hard, look at your picture of Jesus. Visualize his heart bursting into a love that showers the whole world.

Spend at least twenty minutes with your pictures, letting Jesus give you life, letting him raise in you the energies that brought you to life, the energies that let you give life to others.

Notes

1. Dietrich Bonhoeffer, *Ethics* (New York: Macmillan, 1965), p. 296.

2. Gregory Baum, *Man Becoming* (New York: Herder & Herder, 1970).

3. I take this division from Daniel Sullivan's foreword to Abel Jeanniere's *The Anthropology of Sex* (New York: Harper & Row, 1967).

4. *Zohar,* trans. H. Sperling and M. Simon (London: Sancino Press, 1933), vol. 1, p. 286.

5. Edward Hoffman, *The Way of Splendor: Jewish Mysticism and Modern Psychology* (Boulder, Colo.: Shambhala, 1981), pp. 75–84.

6. Maurice Nedoncelle, *Love and the Person,* trans. Sr. Ruth Adelaide (New York: Sheed & Ward, 1966), pp. 18–19.

7. For this exercise and the one following chapter 8, we are indebted to Linda Sabbath.

— VIII —

Prayer in the New Creation

What we see in contemporary society, magnified by the media, is a burst of consciousness development. In the sixties, a great wave of social and political concern erupted, especially among the young. Americans marched, demonstrated, and lay down in the streets for the cause of peace and racial equality. They also tripped on acid and played in the Dionysian fields of the new sexual freedom. Behind all this turmoil was a thirst for expanded consciousness, a defiant rebellion against being a statistic or a digit, a dehumanized cog in the modern industrial wheel.

The Eastern religions, Yoga, Zen, occultism, and the Tibetan Book of the Dead, became part of sophisticated conversation in the seventies. Not merely students, but middle-class businessmen, housewives, nuns, and ministers were into meditation. They found that such disciplines as TM, est, and Silva Mind Control not only relieved anxieties, but opened up areas of the unconscious that they had never suspected, except in their wildest dreams or nightmares. Creative powers were being unleashed: clairvoyance, telepathy, psychokinesis, and out-of-body experiences. Anglican Bishop Pike even wrote a book on communing with the dead through mediums. The "spiritual" life was in vogue.

The eighties have been marked both by conservative materialism and by a countervailing hunger among all social classes for religious experience. They no longer look for it only in traditional forms of worship, but seek living encounters with the living God of Abraham, Isaac, and Jacob, the God whose name could not be spoken. Spiritual seekers have often been disappointed by Western organized religions that tend toward creeds and dogmas, hierarchical structures of authority, and liturgical ritualism. The faithful are desperate to experience God, not as an objective being outside them, but as a divine lover, intimately and immanently present within them at all times.

With so much talk and writing about consciousness expanded to a oneness with God and the universe, we may well ask, just what *is* consciousness? Is it something intellectual that we can acquire by taking a seminar or reading a self-help book, thus raising our mental and spiritual level? Is it merely a higher state of neural functioning? And if so, are there techniques to develop such functioning? Or is it an inner light on which we focus in order to see objects in greater detail, as with bifocals, to aid our limited vision?

Dr. Arthur Diekman defines consciousness as "awareness" rather than the things of which we are aware.[1] Carl Jung uses the analogy of an island to describe the gradual unfolding of our consciousness. The island slowly emerges out of a dark sea. The higher the top of the island, the greater conscious vision is possible, but the island is still totally rooted in the bottom of the sea. A conscious or "spiritual" person would be psychologically open to a clear view of all that is related to his or her own being.

The reason we should have some clear ideas about consciousness is that our level of consciousness affects our personal spiritual lives. Christianity preaches that God is love and that we become both human and godly by living in greater and greater conscious love for God and neighbor. To the extent that our behavior is unconscious, our values are merely ideals, abstracted and removed from our life situations. A low level of conscious awareness of who we are prevents us from moving into oneness with God and neighbor in love. Ultimate, conscious love, a free giving of yourself to another, is the "sacred time," the seventh day of rest, the entrance into the reign of heaven where levels of consciousness continually develop into higher levels of unity in love, along with new awareness of our own uniqueness in that very unity.

To understand growth in prayer as growth through the infusion of the Holy Spirit to new levels of greater consciousness, we should see prayer as an ever purer self-surrender, without attempting to exercise any control over God.

Abraham Heschel, in his beautiful book *The Sabbath,* gives us valuable insights from the Judaic tradition.[2] He shows that what Judaism offers to world religions is the idea of holiness, shifted from the realm of nature and objects to God's eternal self-giving in salvific events.

> You must keep my sabbaths carefully, because the sabbath is a sign between myself and you from generation to generation to show that it is I, Yahweh, who

> sanctify you. You must keep the sabbath, then; it is
> to be held sacred by you.... Work is to be done for six
> days, but the seventh day must be a day of complete
> rest, consecrated to Yahweh. [Exod. 31:13–15]

The rest that allows us to break through the limits of our
individual space and give cosmic meaning to our scattered
labors sweeps us up into God's eternal time and presence. We do not rest from our labors only to regain spent
strength, but we enter into God's "rest," which is the same
as stillness, completion, peace, and harmony. In this rest
is no strife, no fear, no distrust, but only happiness and
eternal life.

In Genesis we read that light was created at the beginning, even before the sun came into existence. This
light allowed human beings to see the world at a glance
from one end to the other. But sin obscured that light,
so that they saw through a glass darkly. Yet certain ones
who have entered into the sabbath rest have shared God's
holiness and presence, seeing the meaningfulness of their
labors. The light of God's intimate presence is seen in the
entrance into deeper prayer, where we move away from the
tyranny of our false self and surrender to God.

God has placed within our consciousness a burning desire to enter into greater union with our creator and thus
with all other human beings, our co-creators. It is a desire
to live forever in God's sacred time, to pray always with
the Holy Spirit who prays within us.

We cannot enter into God's sacred time unless God
leads us into the divine presence (Rom. 8:26–27). It is
only through the Spirit of God's love that we are able to
penetrate into God's innermost mystery and rest in com-

plete communion with God. Only the Spirit "reaches the depths of everything, even the depths of God" (1 Cor. 2:11). Praying "in the Spirit" is to be led by the Spirit into deeper levels of our consciousness and even into the dark desert of our unconscious. It entails stripping ourselves of the false ego that wraps its tentacles around its own created images of God and other persons, refusing to let go. We basically don't want to die to our false hopes and rely only on the security of God's love.

In scriptural language and that of the Eastern Christian mystics of the desert, the heart is the seat of human life, of all that touches us in the depths of our personality: our affections, passions, desires, knowledge, and thoughts. Not our rational head, but our heart is the place where we meet God in an "I–Thou" relationship.[3]

Through discipline and grace we learn to live more and more consciously in the presence of God and to "pray always." A strong desire to live in harmony with God's will is necessary for a life of prayer. Not only should we strongly desire to remain in the presence of God, but such a desire must be accompanied by an uprooting of the false ego, in thought, words, and deed. Paul insists that we should be ready to bring into captivity and obedience to Jesus Christ every thought and every imagination (2 Cor. 10:5). Such watchfulness was well described by St. Basil in the fourth century:

The Christian directs every action, small and great, according to the will of God, performing the action at the same time with care and exactitude, and keeping his thoughts fixed upon the One who gave him the work to do.... We should perform every action as if

> under the eyes of the Lord and think every thought
> as if observed by him,...fulfilling the words of the
> Lord: "I seek not my own will but the will of him
> that sent me, the Father."[4]

When our consciousness of God's loving presence becomes not so much our *doing,* but rather a state of being,
more or less continuous, then we have entered into true
harmony with our real self and are enjoying the seventh
day of rest, in which we even now share in God's eternal
life.

In this prayer of the "heart," the grace of God has
filtered down into our consciousness and has become the
sole determinant of every thought and action. True love
has conquered the heart and we wait in peace to see what
line of action or thought would be most in accord with the
will of God, who has so completely loved us into being.
Such a state of bliss can come only gradually as we struggle in each moment to bring all inordinate attachments or
desires under the one desire to live in God's love and in
unity with all other beings.

Such integration of ourselves in God, the ground of our
being, is reflected in the quality of our prayer. As long as
we are dominated by our false ego, created by our fears and
guilt, we pray to God by asking that we be given what we
think we want, like children in Santa's lap. We believe that
God has permitted or caused something "bad" to happen
in our life. We pray that God have a change of heart.

In such prayer we are creating a god who will serve
our own needs. We want this god to think as we do and
to do our bidding. In such prayer we forget what Jesus
taught us about praying not in vain repetitious prayers,

but acknowledging our broken hearts, our helplessness. To end this obsession with controlling the outside world, we are to go into solitude and shut the door (Matt. 6:5–6).

C. S. Lewis in his *Letters to Malcolm* describes the way to destroy idols and images of God that we have created to maintain ourselves in our false security and illusory control over the God who is a "consuming fire" (Heb. 12:29), if we are to be open to God's fresh and real self-revelation:

> Only God Himself can let the bucket down into the depths in us. And on the other side, He must constantly work as the iconoclast. Every idea of Him we form, He must in mercy shatter. The most blessed result of prayer would be to rise thinking, "But I never knew before. I never dreamed..." I suppose it was at such a moment that Thomas of Aquinas said of all of his theology: "It reminds me of straw."[5]

To allow God's Spirit to strip us of all our idols and knock down our golden calves, we go into the desert of inner poverty. Prayer becomes an "awful waiting," a receptivity to God's word that comes when we are emptied of our own word. Only God's word is true and is capable of transforming our darkness into light, drawing out our true self from the many false masks and false selves that we have built up in our past prayer life in order to maintain our petty grasp on what we want reality to be.

As we descend more deeply within ourselves, God reveals our abyss of nothingness. The more we advance, the more the names and images of God disappear; nothing but God can satisfy. We are in the dark wilderness where God has cut away all the overgrowth so that more fruit can be brought forth (John 15:1). This death to our self-reliance and pride can occur only when we are helpless in darkness, standing before a doorless wall.

We cry out for God to appear in this dark night. Our own powers fail. We cry out in deep, stark faith for God to be revealed. "Lord, Jesus Christ, Son of God, have mercy on me!"

> Instill some joy and gladness into me,
> let the bones you have crushed rejoice again.
> Hide your face from my sins,
> wipe out all my guilt.
>
> [Ps. 51:8–9]

The acknowledgment of emptiness must be made before the vessel can be filled. In prayer we are dispossessed of the self we have so long accepted as us. The shell is cracking and the inner seed, made according to the image and likeness of Jesus Christ, is ready to burst into flower.

Such prayer cannot be taught. Like love itself, it can only be experienced. And when we experience such union with God and others in loving prayer, we will not need to speak about it, only to live it. The Spirit of the risen Jesus pours into the deepest levels of our consciousness (Rom. 5:5). We know that we know. Our lives are transformed. We know and act in union of love with all persons we meet. God is discovered inside each moment, loving us and transforming us into who we always have been in God's love.

To gain this knowing, we enter into the "cloud of unknowing," experiencing God in luminous darkness as we see our own inner poverty and sickness. We are moving into the reign of heaven and are blessed because now in our honesty and authenticity we are becoming "poor in spirit" (Matt. 5:3). The prodigal son has returned home, after having separated himself so long from the Father's home and love, out of desire to be independent from his Father. Returning home, he no longer feels himself to be under the law of a tyrant, but is liberated by forgiveness, so that he can return love for love. Love has healed his desire to live in separation and loneliness.

As we move out into the world after experiencing deep prayer, we find that the divine Word surrounds everything and everyone. We see the same world we saw before, but now we see it clearly in the light of eternity.

Our prayer now becomes one of resisting any activity that is strictly our own. We become actively receptive in surrendering ourselves to God's activity. No longer do we ask for prayers to be answered by God on our behalf. Praise alone comes from our heart, for we understand that God reads it and knows every need before we could even ask. So why ask? Why use words at all? With God now so intimately present to us, we wait in silence. We *are* in God's holy presence. No anxiety troubles our peace; we truly know now that God loves us infinitely and unconditionally. We trust more deeply in God's love, abandoning ourselves like children to the sacrament of the present moment. Now that we have put on the mind of Christ, we love as he loves. Our ego with its attachments and delusions drops away.

What is important at this new level of contemplative prayer is to avoid conceptualizing God's presence in order to possess it more securely, returning to the flesh pots of Egypt, our false ego. The idolatry of self-worship is one of the greatest dangers of contemplative prayer. To reach this point where God's presence is non-conceptually experienced, and then to cling to it selfishly, wanting the psychic effects of this state for ourselves, is to create an idol. Further growth is stunted by such narcissism, which is a movement away from reality to the world of shadows and nonbeing. Christian prayer seeks "the self in God," not God in the self.

We cannot *escape* from a material world in order to find God only in sacred places and occupations. We need to *inscape* to enter directly into the heart of matter and find there the heart of uncreated energies of God, which set material creation in motion. Matter, work in the world, our contemporary history, sex, and marriage must be seen positively as drenched with God's loving, creative power. The material world is now the help God intended it to be when God said of creation that it was good (Gen. 1:31). The Kingdom of God is within us; we see ourselves as cells of Christ's Body. The active and contemplative lives are now a single life of loving God within us and everywhere around us.

Our disparate activities seem suspended as we enter into a tranquility that brings us a sense of oneness with God. Nikos Kazantzakis in his *Report to Greco* describes the moving away from discursive meditation to a general mood of oneness with God and all things in God: "I saw the world as a tree, a gigantic poplar, and myself as a green leaf clinging to a branch with my slender stalk. When God's wind blew, I hopped and danced, together with the entire tree."[6] In such deep, wordless, self-forgetful prayer, we seem to be standing inside our real self, inside our deepest reality, communing with God as if we were standing also *in* God, loving God without words or images.

An expanded consciousness in contemplative prayer

begins as we enter deeply into the material world around us, for we see "only one Christ; he is everything and he is in everything" (Col. 3:11). The "unified field" Einstein vainly looked for in the world of phenomena exists only in Christ-consciousness. The beginning of our search is our end, and the end is the beginning. Love, like all energies, never stands still but moves in the circuit of the tiniest electron as it does in the sweep of the farthest nebula. It is the umbilical cord between us and the universe.

EXERCISE

Heart-to-Heart Prayer

Make yourself comfortable in a chair or sitting on the floor, before your picture of Christ. Take as long as you need to center yourself on this picture, excluding all distractions. Clear your mind of words, thoughts, and images. You are having a heart-to-heart talk with Jesus. Your presence is all that's needed, for he knows you love him. No words are necessary.

Focus on the heart of Christ. Know its energies are pouring into *your* heart. What you see with your physical eyes, with your brain, doesn't matter. All that matters is that you know your heart is Christ's, that you want to love as he does. Breathe in "Jesus," breathe out "Lord," knowing that these words can evoke the energies that empower the whole universe. As you did in Exercise VII, raise your sexual energies to your heart and offer them to their Maker, God. See the faces of all those you love, all those who have given you love. Take them into your heart as you breathe in and breathe out, giving them back to God, from whom they came.

As you breathe deeply, your attention still focused on the heart area, consciously let go of the burdens you have laid on your heart — worry, self-doubt, fear of being unloved, of not being thought "good enough." The heart is at the core of the body and is the center that drives your divinely given energies through the stem of your body until they flower in your mind and in your life.

As you hear and feel the heart become quiet, beating more slowly; also quiet your mind, letting it rest in the presence of God. Let your heart, your pulse, your breath, beat on the shore of God, steady as the sea's waves. Images of all the scattered pieces of your life, even images of Christ, fall away as you let go of all the words you want to tell him but now have no need to. If you have a hard time stilling the static, try just listening to your heart and breath again.

When you have cleared your mind of all noise, try adding a fourth element to your breathing pattern (intake – pause – outbreath): let the lungs rest empty a moment at the end of the cycle. Concentrating on this stillness may help you stay still, but if it's a distraction, just let the breath come and go naturally. *Be* in God's presence, having no agendas, no ideas, no desires. You are not trying to change yourself or anyone else, to achieve any goal, know any truth. With Christ, you are in the Father and the Father in you. You pass over the face of God like a cloud over the sun, the divine light spreading through you. Let this light and silence grow in your life as you share with the world the love you have become.

Notes

1. Arthur J. Deikman, "The Meaning of Everything," unpublished manuscript, University of Colorado Medical School, 1970, cited by Dr. John O. Meany, *Psychology of "Personal Theology and Prayer,"* no. 2, vol. 28 (1973), pp. 340–350.

2. Abraham J. Heschel, *The Sabbath* (New York: Farrar, Straus & Giroux, 1951).

3. See A. Guillaumont, "Le sens du coeur dans l'antiquité," in *Le Coeur: Etudes carmélitaines* (Paris: Desclée de Brouwer, 1950), pp. 41–88.

4. St. Basil, "Regulae fusius tractatae," *PG* 31:920C-921B.

5. C. S. Lewis, *Letters to Malcolm* (New York: Harcourt, Brace & World, 1964), p. 84.

6. Nikos Kazantzakis, *Report to Greco* (New York: Simon and Schuster, 1958), p. 280.

— IX —

Transforming Our World

Mother Teresa of Calcutta tells a story that reveals clearly the relation of prayer to service in the world.

"During the Mass," I said, "you saw that the priest touched the body of Christ with great love and tenderness. When you touch the poor today, you too will be touching the body of Christ. Give them that same love and tenderness." When they returned several hours later, the new sister came up to me, her face shining with joy. "I have been touching the Body of Christ for three hours," she said. I asked her what she had done. "Just as we arrived, the sister brought in a man covered with maggots. He had been picked up from a drain. I have been taking care of him, I have been touching Christ. I knew it was him," she said.[1]

In the suffering and poor, as Jesus promised us, we encounter him just as we do in prayer.

The depth of our transformation from false ego to true self through God's love can be measured by the love we show others. Those who meet God intimately within their hearts and share God's oneness with the creation, must be concerned with the cries of suffering brothers and sisters wherever in the world they may be victims of disease, oppression, wars, or natural calamities.

Can we be unmoved before the human pain and anguish heaped upon so many sufferers? Have we truly left the darkness of egoism for the light of God's self-giving love if we are unconcerned with the one billion people who are malnourished and destitute?

Thirty million landless and penniless refugees in underdeveloped countries are seriously ill and have no hope of economic survival even if they should get well. Of the twenty-eight million blind people in the world, twenty-four million are in the Third World, suffering mostly from river blindness and vitamin A deficiency, both preventable if people cared enough to help. The cost of controlling malaria, sleeping sickness, and river blindness would be about three billion dollars, equivalent to half of what the world spends on armaments every day.[2] The money spent on junk food, cigarettes, and alcohol in the U.S. alone could save nearly all the children in the Third World from blindness.

The social sin of ignoring the suffering of others has always been with us, but we see it more clearly in today's society than ever before. In an earlier, less affluent, less conscious age, we could not have known about the extent of the suffering in the world, let alone have felt responsibility for relieving it. We could not have known that thousands of children in this country are being sexually abused for the profit of those who own them. With the birth of the social sciences, our society's mechanisms were exposed. We could see that poverty, hunger, and ignorance are not a matter of bad luck or the punishment for bad behavior, but largely the result of socio-economic inequity. Such misery becomes all the more glaring in a society of abundance like ours.

If we are to help others, we must focus all our attention on seeing them as ourselves. Our personal practice must be service. As Christ washed the feet of his friends, so must we. Because we live in a democracy, we are given legal and political opportunities to do more than an occasional good deed. Our second and larger responsibility is to work for a more humane distribution of wealth. In America, even a poor man can become president, so the slogans claim, yet our last five presidents have been millionaires. The same social structures that encourage our obsession with self and pleasure, also perpetuate an economic inequity — 1 percent of America's population controls 70 percent of the country's wealth. Equality of opportunity, once a given in our society, is now limited. We take care of ourselves and ignore the unemployed black teenagers, the women struggling to support families abandoned by fathers, old men wandering homeless in the city streets. Our false egos found the sinful status quo merely "business as usual," but our transformed selves cannot, knowing that each individual is responsible for the whole Body.

Through the mass media all of us are now aware of evils known only to a few in earlier eras. In the United States, an informed people rose up and stopped a vicious war conducted by their government against the Vietnamese. Above-ground nuclear testing was stopped by a protest of individuals around the world, crying out as with one voice, "Enough!" As the tide of genocide, oppression, and poverty rises, we are overwhelmed, unsure we have the strength to roll it back. Our unconscious is loaded with guilt over the sufferings of those we see nightly on our television screens, whose cries of pain are perhaps heard at a deeper level, in our collective unconscious. Worldwide economic problems, nuclear destruction, mass starvation, and ecological ruin are all troubles too vast to be solved merely by electing a stronger president or a more moral Congress. Only a transformation of ourselves into a potent, unified Body of Christ can accomplish the task at hand.

Too often we hide from the world's pain, insulating ourselves with expensive escapes. Some of us turn to a comforting religion that promises a heaven in the next life if we do not become too preoccupied with this one. Most of us claim like the German neighbors of the smoking crematoria that we don't know what's going on and if we knew, we couldn't change it. Meanwhile, ignoring all the wisdom of this world, a Mother Teresa went to the Calcutta slums with five rupees in her pocket, and quietly transformed the lives of thousands. What is the convinced Christian to do? To answer, we must look at the Christ of the Gospels, not sugaring his example or his message with our own excuses and agendas.

Responding with the fullness and harmony of his body, mind, and spirit, Jesus moved in freedom before the loving gaze of the Father, who was well-pleased at what he saw. He respected the traditions of his race and religion but did not worship them as absolutes. He loved all human beings, especially the despised, the maimed, the oppressed, the prostitutes, publicans, lepers, and demon-possessed. He was kind and gentle toward those sufferers, pouring into them the healing love of the Father.

Jesus identified himself with the outcasts of his time,

the *Amharez,* the despised "people of the land" of the Old Testament, and thus incurred the wrath of the politicians and religious leaders of his society. He was patient with such leaders, answering their questions. But he made it clear that human beings were more important than the sabbath, especially if any person were suffering unjustly. He took liberties with the Law, healing on the sabbath, allowing his hungry disciples to eat on a fast day. He condemned religious leaders who used religion for their own selfish interests and ı rotested the burdens laid upon the poor. Jesus set all people free from the Law but only so that they could fulfill it, so that they could love all human beings through the power of God. St. Paul well understood Christ's message when he wrote: "If you are led by the Spirit, no law can touch you" (Gal. 5:18). The Spirit of Jesus brings us into the new law, which is to "carry each other's troubles and fulfill the law of Christ" (Gal. 6:2).

In order to enter into the Kingdom of God, Jesus says we must love one another as he has loved us (John 15:12). Jesus not only denounced the evils coming from social and religious structures that kept the poor oppressed and dehumanized, but he announced and effected the new order, his new creation-in-the-making. Men and women were to be awakened from their sleep, opening their eyes to their oneness with a new Body, knit together by God's love flowing within them and among them. While he was on earth, Jesus healed the sick and the broken, the diseased, the mentally unbalanced, those caught up in selfishness and lack of love. Nor did he consider those whom he healed as healthy only when their sins were forgiven or when their bodies were restored to physical health. It was the whole person that Jesus loved and to whom he ministered in order to build a whole, harmonious society, the Body of himself, his church.

The early Christians were convinced that those who were in Christ were already new creations and that God was calling them to be cooperators and "reconcilers," as Paul calls anyone who has "put on" the new self (2 Cor. 5:17–18; Eph. 4:22–25). The words of Thomas Merton aptly summarize the belief and conduct of the primitive church: "It is only in assuming full responsibility for our world, for our lives and for ourselves that we can be said to live really for God."[3]

That ancient apostolic writing, the Didache, gives us the common teaching and practice of the early Christian church: "Do not turn away from the needy; rather, share everything with your brother, and do not say, 'It is private property.' If you are sharers in what is incorruptible, how much more so in things that perish."[4] St. Ambrose gives the doctrine that was shared by the Western and Eastern Fathers:

> The Lord our God willed that this earth should be the common property of all mankind, and so He offered its produce for all to enjoy; but man's avarice distributed the right to its possession.[5]

As the Fathers understood, one cannot justify possessing great wealth by claiming "poverty of spirit" in one's detachment from riches while enjoying them. Complete detachment is sharing one's wealth with the needy. The early church declared that sharing the wealth is not merely a generous condescension on the part of the rich, but an acknowledgment that the poor have a right to receive a share of wealth that belongs to God, Father of all.

When German students volunteered to rebuild an English cathedral after World War II, an argument arose as to how to repair a large statue of Jesus. The outstretched arms were stumps; the hands could not be found. Instead of fashioning new ones, the students decided to leave the statue as it was, adding an inscription that reads, "Christ has no hands but ours." Only by the work of our hands, busy with everyday life, can the Kingdom of God be built. The decision to take part in this cosmic work is up to us.

George Mangatt describes the Kingdom of God as not purely an otherworldly reality to be realized only in

> the future, but something that has effectively entered into history, transforming human existence.... Jesus conceived his mission as an integral liberation of the whole human person; that is why he went about healing the sick, feeding the hungry, freeing the possessed; that is why he fought the injustices of the Jewish aristocracy.[6]

Jesus acted as if the human race were already one, because in his eyes, God's eyes, it was and is. It is we who are blind to that oneness, allowing other members of our body to be starved, tortured, and degraded, not understanding that we too are being diminished.

To the degree that human beings follow Jesus Christ, God's new creation is already taking form. In Christian countries, slavery no longer exists, women are not chattel, child labor is prohibited. Justice and equality, the right to pursue one's individual happiness rather than merely to serve the state, are ideals woven into the social fabric, even though the garment often tears, and in places like Latin

America, is rent to rags. Only our constant attention to Jesus' Spirit of love will bring about the new Jerusalem in every area of human life.

The transforming of today's society into a world of justice, peace, and love can come about only when we "carry each other's troubles and fulfill the law of Christ" (Gal. 6:2). In order to enter the Kingdom of God, Jesus says we must love one another as he has loved us (John 15:12) — meaning sacrifice, meaning readiness to lay down one's life, meaning death to self.

Jesus commissioned his first disciples not merely to announce the good news about the coming of the Kingdom of God, but to bring his healing love and power to all humankind.

> Go out to the whole world; proclaim the Good News to all creation.... These are the signs that will be associated with believers: ... they will lay their hands on the sick, who will recover. [Mark 16:16–18]

We too are his disciples. Will we hold our ears or will we hear his call?

Each of us will respond differently to Christ's command to share ourselves and our possessions with others who have less than we do, depending upon our charisms and our "place" within the Body of Christ, the church. But all of us are called to be completely open to sharing ourselves so that others can grow to their fullness in God. Pope Paul addressed his apostolic exhortation *Evangelica Testificatio* to Catholic religious on the matter of poverty, violence, and justice, but it speaks to us all. In it he wrote that the cry of the poor must be answered by serious Christians: "That cry must, first of all, bar you from whatever would be a compromise with any form of social injustice."[7] Not only priests and nuns must hear the cry of the poor; the rest of us must hear it too. Giving money to the missions once a year does not buy rest for our consciences. As long as the suffering goes on, as long as the Body bleeds, we ourselves are dying. To live, we must heal the wound.

All Christians are called to live by the Beatitudes, which define the conduct of the new people of Israel. We all cannot spread the Kingdom of God exactly as Dr. Albert Schweitzer did in his work among the suffering and oppressed Africans, as did Mahatma Gandhi or Mother Teresa in India or Archbishop Oscar Romero in El Salvador. Wherever we are, through our love for one other person, we come to learn that true love cannot be turned inward or even God-ward in an exclusive way. It breaks out toward a larger community where we find our love growing as we take responsibility for suffering human beings, in whom Jesus shows himself to us. We give away God's love to the world according to our talents and state in life, *but we must give something.* The anguished cry for justice that rises from human beings around the world must rise simultaneously from the depths of our hearts as we struggle under their burdens, weeping with those who weep, as Jesus told us to do.

As the love of God more and more fills us, we go forth sacrificing ourselves to the other members of the Body, giving them what God has given us. As we were forgiven, so we forgive, aware that we are called to be an instrument of peace, reconciling people with God and with the world around them. No one is a stranger to us, only a brother or sister. We stand between the suffering Body of Christ and God; with outstretched arms we humbly offer the high-

priest prayer of Christ to his Father that all might be one
as he and the Father are one (John 17:23).

Not only do we become prophetic examples of humankind's oneness in Christ, but we become a leaven of reform
in the social structures that cramp the freedom of other
human beings to live up to their God-given potential. As
Jesus was not a mere prophet but a still point on the turning world, through which God's healing cosmic energies
unite him with every one of us, so we must be focal points
for divine creative energies that will bring into being the
New Israel, the Kingdom of God.

The church has always known that its members and
leaders must work for human development and freedom
as they spread the Kingdom of God on earth. Instead
of fleeing social responsibility, we must stay in the world,
following Jesus, who was not ashamed to be born in a
stable and die on a cross. We, as members of Christ's
Body, carry the life-bearing and glory-raising Jesus in the
chalice of this world, feeding him to his lambs, watering his
buried grains of wheat with the blood that will resurrect
them, Christ's and ours.

As we leave behind our egotistical notions of a merely
individual bodily resurrection and see ourselves as already
risen in the whole Body of Christ, the world will look different to us. No longer will we see it in the light of the Fall,
but in the light of Christ risen, for the world is God's, not
the devil's. The resurrection of Jesus becomes the force
that spirals the whole universe back into the arms of God
from whom it was first born. What happened to Jesus
in the Resurrection will happen to us, to the human family, to all creation. Christ is the *Alpha* and the *Omega*,
at once the center of the material world and its destina-

tion, recapitulating the entire cosmos back to the Father: "and all things to be reconciled through Him and for him, everything in heaven and everything on earth" (Col. 1:20).

Yet God lets us help. The humility of God! God stakes the gathering of all things into himself on our weak cooperation. Simone Weil dramatically put it: "A victim of misfortune is lying in the road, half-dead with hunger. God pities him but cannot send him bread. But I am here and luckily I am not God. I can give him a piece of bread. It is my one point of superiority over God."

We are privileged to be a part of Christ's Body, a true leaven that rises in the bread of creation "christi-fying" all areas of created existence, bringing it under the wings of Christ, who so longed to spread those wings over Jerusalem like a mother hen leaning over her chicks (Matt. 23:37; Luke 13:35). The cosmic Christ is moving creation to fulfillment, shaping it to his divine form. Ultimately the universe will not be annihilated as materialistic science tells us, but will be transformed. As we must be changed by many deaths to our false egos and birthed into our true identity, the dark corruption of our ego-mangled world must dissolve into light. We do not merely return to our primitive state of Eden at play in the fields of the Lord, but become the gardeners, unlocking every clod, every lump of matter, that it might grow, bear fruit, nourish.

If we are guided by the experience of the Resurrection of Jesus in our *now* moment, we will see that we are already "becoming" a part of the total, glorified Christ. As the Resurrection of Jesus is the marriage of God and humankind, so is our transformation in the Holy Spirit. It is not we who live, we with our posturing false egos, but Christ who lives in us. Finally, at the consummate Omega

of the material world, wrenched into glory by the birthing
hands of God, there is only Christ: "he is everything and
he is in everything" (Col. 3:11).

EXERCISE

Sharing Yourself

Go through your local newspapers and magazines until you
find a picture of a person living in real poverty. When you
find one that strikes you, tape it on the wall next to the
crucifix, icon, or holy picture before which you customarily
pray.

At the beginning of your meditation, take a few moments to study this picture. How does the person seem to
be feeling? How would *you* feel, in his or her place?

- If you were standing next to the person in your picture and wanted to give the same comfort you would
  give Christ himself, what would you say?

- Invent a brief dialogue with this person, asking what
  he to she wants you to do.

- Keeping your eyes on this face, imagine yourself in
  the picture looking out, asking for what you need.

- Now imagine the face to be the face of Christ. Hear
  him saying to you: "What you do for this child of
  mine, you have done for me."

- Put the picture of your person in your wallet, not in
  the photo section, but with your money. Whenever
  you reach into the wallet and see your person, ask

yourself what financial help you are giving people like him or her. Remind yourself that God has given you money so that you can share it with others.

Notes

1. Mother Teresa, "The Poor in Our Midst," in *New Covenant* (Ann Arbor, Mich., January 1977), cited by William Johnston in *The Inner Eye of Love* (London: Collins, 1978), pp. 26–27.

2. ICROSS (International Community for the Relief of Starvation and Suffering) is a realistic, practical way to be directly involved. An international board of specialists help interested parties throughout the world to become aware of the issues involved in poverty and ways we can help to meet the most tragic needs. Its headquarters in the United States is at 238 Old Town Road, Southampton, NY 11968; Director: Dr. Kenneth B. Cairns, M.D.

3. Thomas Merton: *Contemplation in a World of Action* (Garden City, New York: Doubleday, 1971), p. 54.

4. "Didache," in *Ancient Christian Writers*, ed. J. Quasten and J. Plumpe, trans. J. A. Keist (Baltimore: Newman, 1967), vol. 6, p. 17.

5. St. Ambrose, "Expositio in Ps. CXVIII," 8th Sermon, 22, *PL* 15:1503.

6. G. Mangatt, "Jesus and Service," in *Jeevadhara* (Alleppey, India), no. 22, 1972, pp. 276–277.

7. Pope Paul VI, *The Teachings of Pope Paul VI* (Washington: U.S. Bishops Conference, 1972), p. 384.

A Last Meditation

So you close the door to the house of your heart, where now you live with God. But suddenly, in a burst of light as when empty space lit up at the birth of matter, a whole cosmos opens around you, prodigal with stars, bright seas, shining swarms of life. You swing in a radiant web of bodies being spun by God. When you open your lips to taste the light, to cry your love, you find you have no words, and at last, you sing silence.

To obtain an audio cassette tape guiding the meditations suggested in this book, send $10 with your name and address to:

> Christ Consciousness
> Box 4152
> Milpas Station
> Santa Barbara, CA 93105

One-day workshops to train facilitators to teach contemplative prayer can be arranged on request.